Big Things Happen
When You Do the
Little Things Right

Also by the Author

BIG THINGS

Happen When
You Do the
Little Things
Right

A FIVE-STEP PROGRAM
TO TURN YOUR DREAMS
INTO REALITY

DON GABOR

PRIMA PUBLISHING

PRIMA PUBLISHING and colophon are registered trademarks of Prima Communications, Inc.

Library of Congress Cataloging-in-Publication Data
Gabor, Don.
    Big things happen when you do the little things right :
    a five-step program to turn your dreams into reality / Don Gabor.
       p.   cm.
    Includes bibliographical references and index.
    ISBN 0-7615-0535-0
    1. Success   I. Title.
BJ1611.G29   1997
158.1—dc21   97-3923
                                            CIP

98 99 00 01 HH 10 9 8 7 6 5 4 3
Printed in the United States of America

HOW TO ORDER
Single copies may be ordered from Prima Publishing, P.O. Box 1260BK, Rocklin, CA 95677; telephone (916) 632-4400. Quantity discounts are available. On your letterhead, include information concerning the intended use of the books and the number of books you wish to purchase.

VISIT US ONLINE AT WWW.PRIMAPUBLISHING.COM

To my mother and father

Contents

Contents

Step Five: Build on Your Success

Acknowledgments

I WANT TO THANK several people for making this book possible. My deepest appreciation goes to my wife, Eileen Cowell, for her unflagging encouragement, masterful editing, and support throughout this project. I owe my agent, Sheree Bykofsky, and her colleague Janet Rosen a debt of gratitude for their feedback, hard work, and their skill in negotiating this book contract. Special thanks to my father, who impressed upon me that if I am going to do something, I must be sure to do it right. His attitude of persistence toward work and achievement continue to inspire me to do all I can. I also want to thank my mother for her ongoing encouragement and support. She told me as a child that I could do anything I wanted if I worked hard enough. (As it has turned out, she was, for the most part, right.) Finally, I could not have finished this long project without the constant companionship of my faithful office cats, Sophie, Callie, Sylvester, Sobro, and Amber.

Introduction

I OFTEN BEGIN MY "Big Things Happen" workshops with the following experiment. I wait until everyone sits and gets comfortable. Then I tell them to pick up their belongings and find another seat at another table. You ought to hear the groans and see the nasty looks I get! But after a few moments of hesitation, most people get up to make a move. I then say, "Stop, you can stay where you are." They all flop back into their seats with a big sigh of relief.

Next, I pose this question: "Many of you were obviously annoyed when I told you to find another seat. Why was that?" Some people say that they were comfortable and didn't want to move. Others say they like sitting next to their friends. Some point out that they can see better from where they are. A few people say that they don't like anyone telling them where to sit. Most agree that they could change seats if they had to. They also say that the closer the new seat was to their original, the easier it would be to make the change.

Then I ask, "If making a little change such as moving to a different seat in the same room causes you discomfort, how would a big change make you feel?" Everyone laughs and gets my point: If making small changes is troublesome, making a big change may seem impossible.

Most of us desire success in our personal and professional lives, yet we are often unwilling or unable to make the necessary changes to accomplish our goals. The reason is simple. Making big changes in our lives is scary and often difficult. I believe that the secret to achieving your dreams is to take many small, well-planned steps with a specific big goal as a target.

How This Book Can Help You

Do you want to make personal or professional changes, accomplish ambitious goals, and fulfill your lifelong dreams? This book will help you:

> ◆ change your career ◆ find a new job ◆ build a savings account ◆ start a business ◆ move to a new home ◆ get a college degree ◆ find a mate ◆ improve your relationships ◆ get a divorce ◆ build a house ◆ write a book ◆ learn a foreign language ◆ master a new computer program ◆ get a promotion ◆ market an invention ◆ improve your body ◆ sail around the world ◆ climb a mountain ◆ run a marathon ◆ or achieve any other goal you desire—if you are willing to commit to it

How to Use This Book

Big Thing Happen When You Do the Little Things Right is based on skills, attitudes, and exercises that have helped me and many other people achieve small and large goals. This book presents a concise five-step plan for achieving your midterm and long-term goals. The process goes like this:

Commitment + Planning + Action + Persistence =
Accomplishing Your Dream

Each chapter presents vital information, dozens of examples, and specific things you can do to accomplish the small steps and midterm goals that lead to accomplishing your dreams. The unique Problem-Solving Strategy Exercise and follow-up at the end of each chapter offer you a hands-on opportunity to apply each skill you learn. In addition, each chapter closes with a Little Things Checklist and a brief description of what's to come in the following chapter.

I encourage you to use a separate notebook in which to work the exercises in the book. As you complete each exercise, you will be learning skills you can use to transform your dreams into reality. With focused effort and a willingness to take a few risks, you'll be on the road to achieving your long-term goals.

Are you ready to get what you want from life and make your most ambitious dreams come true? If you say yes, then take your first step right now. Make a commitment to yourself to read this book and do the exercises; they are fun, instructive, and insightful. By taking one step at a time, keeping your eyes on your long-term goal, and putting out the effort, you'll see that you *can* make big things happen when you do the little things right.

Step One

COMMIT TO A BIG GOAL

"Until one is committed, there is hesitancy, the chance to draw back, always ineffectiveness.... Whatever you can do or dream, you can begin it. Boldness has genius, power, and magic in it. Begin it now."

—Johann Wolfgang von Goethe (1749–1832),
German poet and dramatist

1

Where Do You Want to
Be in Five Years?

"There is only one success—to be able to spend your life in your own way."

—Christopher Darlington Morley (1890–1957),
American author

WHEN I TURNED twenty-one, my father asked me, "Don, what is your five-year plan?"

"Five-year plan!" I gasped. "I don't even know what I'm going to be doing in the next five minutes! How in the world am I supposed to know what I'm going to be doing in five years?"

He asked, "Well, what do you want?"

"I just want to be happy."

"What will make you happy?"

"I don't know!" I said, and that ended our conversation—at least for the time being.

At that point in my life I didn't know what I wanted, when I wanted it, nor did I have even the slightest idea of what would make me happy. Like most young people, I figured I would try different things, and when I hit upon what made me happy, I would know it. And, as with most people, I had a mixture of successes and failures.

Eventually I discovered the concept that my father had been trying to communicate to me years before. If I know what I want and when I want it, I can then work backward to achieve my objective. By having a goal fixed in mind, I can identify what I need to be doing three years, two years, one year, six months, one month, one week—even one day—from today to accomplish this goal.

For example, in 1973, after substitute teaching a few months as an elementary school music teacher, I dreamed of getting a full-time teaching job. The problem was, I needed to go back to school to earn my permanent teaching certification. My first step in achieving that long-term goal was to find out how long this process would take. Then I worked backward to identify each step leading to my goal. Bingo! Two years later (with a few bumpy spots and some help along the way), I had earned my elementary teaching certificate and found a full-time position as an elementary school music teacher.

Decide What You Want and Make It Happen

"The young tell you what they are doing, the old what they have done, and everyone else what they are going to do."
—Laurence J. Peter (1919–1990),
Canadian writer; author of *The Peter Principle*

Are you waiting for something wonderful to happen to you? When someone asks what you want most in life, does your mind go blank as you sigh, "To win the lottery"? If I asked you how you would describe your own success, would you say, "I'll know it when I see it"? In other words, does your philosophy of life go something like, "I believe in fate. Whatever happens, happens"?

If these examples describe your way of thinking, then you are not alone. Surveys of adults consistently show that only one person in ten identifies long-term goals. The remaining nine people passively drift through life, taking the changes as they come. This is fine if you have nowhere in particular to go. However, if you dream of doing bigger things, a step-by-step approach will make it possible. The first step on the path to success is to define your long-term goals.

See Long-Term Goals in Terms of the "Big Picture"

A long-term goal is like the north star: It is a constant factor or point of orientation that gives you a destination and a sense direction. A long-term goal is the "big picture" or the long view of what you want to accomplish. To put a long-term goal into perspective, think of it as an endeavor that takes anywhere from six months to five years to accomplish. For example, long-term goals that take six months to achieve might be learning how to drive a car or finding a new job. Long-term goals that might take five years or more to achieve could be building a successful small business or earning a college degree.

Your long-term goals—whether they are to retire at fifty, to become a concert violinist, or to raise a family—focus your efforts. Without clearly defined goals, there is good chance that you'll waste time and miss opportunities to fulfill your personal or professional ambitions. It is true that life offers no guarantees, but if you have a long-term goal, you have decided your destination before setting out upon the journey.

When he was twelve years old, a boy named Steve Jobs telephoned Bill Hewlett, the president and a founder of Hewlett-Packard, and asked for some spare computer parts so he could build his own computer. Even at an early age, he knew the power of setting long-term goals. Steve Jobs went on to be a cofounder of Apple Computer. And he didn't stop there.

How Can You Turn Your Dreams into Reality?

"Dreams are the touchstones of our characters."
—Henry David Thoreau (1817–1862),
American essayist

Do you still dream of achieving great things? If you are like many adults, your ambitions may be growing cold on the back burner. Maybe it's been so long since you thought about your hopes and dreams that you don't even remember what they are. So take a little step and identify your lifelong dreams again. They are vital to your success because dreams fuel your motivation. With commitment, planning, and action your dreams can grow from attainable goals to reality.

As a youngster I loved to start conversations with strangers because it was fun and interesting. I never knew where the conversations would lead or when I might make a new friend, but I could count on them being entertaining. One of my favorite high school teachers gave me my nickname, "Gabby." He often said that if I could talk for a living I'd have my "dream" job. That was when I first dreamed of getting paid to talk. Today I'm a professional speaker, communications trainer, and author. My dream job has become a reality. But first I had to identify what I wanted to achieve.

I also used to dream of becoming a veterinarian. However, when I faced the stark reality of poor college math and chemistry grades, I realized that my talents lay elsewhere. Even so, today I play the home vet with our five cats and a box turtle. In this situation, my dream of becoming a vet turned into a rewarding hobby.

Another dreamer, Bill Marriott, Sr., wanted to create a successful chain of hotels throughout the world. He describes his dream this way: "I started out with three general ideas in mind. One was to render friendly service to our guests. The second was to provide quality food at a fair price. The third was to work as hard as I could, day and night, to make a profit." Marriott knew what he wanted to achieve; today, his successful hotels are established throughout the world.

Add Details to Your Big Picture Goals

Do you want to be rich? Do you want to be happy? Do you want glory and fame? As fantasies, these are fine, but as goals they lack a vital component: They are too vague. Define your long-term goals with as much detail as possible. *Be specific.* Keep asking yourself the question: What do I want to achieve? Here are some specific ways to answer to that question:

♦ I want to earn $100,000 a year by the time I am fifty so I can retire and travel through every state in the country.

♦ I want to read one book a month so I can improve my understanding of the world around me.

- ◆ I want to get a job I enjoy in the computer industry within six months.

- ◆ I want to learn to play the guitar so I can perform professionally within three years.

- ◆ I want to save $50 per week so I will have $10,000 in the next four years to make a down payment on my dream home.

- ◆ I want to earn a college degree in the culinary arts so I can open my own restaurant.

Knowing where you want to go is the first big step. The clearer your picture of your long-term goal, the easier it is to identify the big and little steps it takes to achieve it. When you know your destination, your chances of getting there are better than if you start the journey with only a vague idea of where you want to end up. As the great baseball legend Yogi Berra said, "If you don't know where you are going, you might wind up somewhere else."

LITTLE EXERCISES THAT GET BIG RESULTS
Number One:
Start Your Dream Machine

Problem-Solving Strategy:
Defining Your Objectives
This strategy helps you define your dreams as worthwhile and achievable goals.

What's the problem? Getting over obstacles and making your dreams come true is difficult unless you clearly define your objectives. You begin the problem-solving and goal-setting process when you put your dreams into words.

What to do: The purpose of this exercise is to identify some of your long-term goals and their benefits. On the following page, write a few words inside each oval describing different goals you would like to achieve. Then add a few words to the lines outside each oval that describe the benefits of achieving your goals. I have done one example for you.

FOLLOW-UP

You probably dream of achieving many things, but turning your aspirations into reality requires effort, concentration, desire, and stamina. Therefore, your next step is to choose *one* dream that you want to focus on—at least for the exercises in this book. If you're not sure which one to pursue, that's okay.

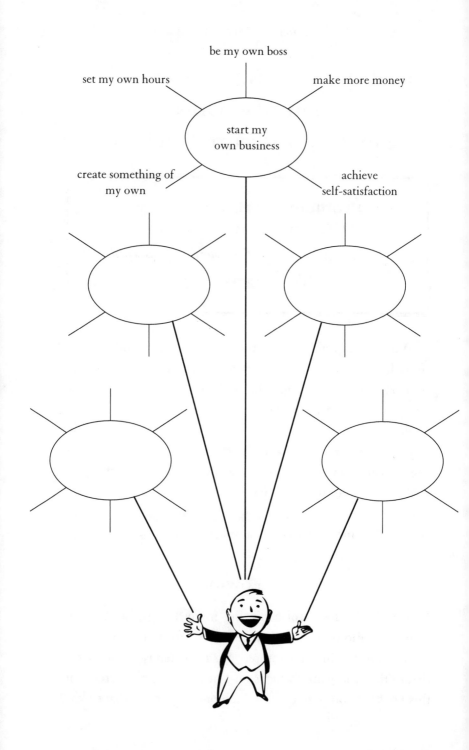

be my own boss

set my own hours

make more money

start my
own business

create something of
my own

achieve
self-satisfaction

Pick the dream that seems most worthwhile and fun to you. Then, as you complete the exercises at the end of each chapter, you'll know what to do when you settle on the dream you truly want to accomplish.

For the sake of the exercises in this book, the big dream I want to focus on is:

_____

_____

_____

_____

_____

_____

_____

_____

_____

_____

_____

_____

_____

_____

_____

_____

_____

_____

Little Things Checklist

Here are some questions to consider when thinking about your long-term goals. The answers will help you clarify where you want to go and what you want to do when you get there.

✔ Which of my accomplishments am I most proud of?

✔ What hobbies give me the most satisfaction?

✔ What capabilities do I have that could make life better for someone else?

✔ Based on my past failures and successes, what might be my next goal?

✔ What have I been putting off that I would still like to do?

✔ What goal would bring me great personal satisfaction?

WHAT'S NEXT?

Now that you've zeroed in on a long-term goal, you're ready to move ahead to chapter two. Your next step is identifying your motivation.

2

Why in the World
Are You Doing This?

"If one advances confidently in the direction of his dreams, and endeavors to live the life which he has imagined, he will meet with a success unexpected in common hours."

—Henry David Thoreau (1817–1862),
American essayist

DO YOU START and stop big projects at the drop of a hat? Are you fired up at the beginning of a major endeavor, only to quit when the going gets tough or you get bored? Have you tried one career after another but still cannot seem to find a job that makes you happy? Do your parents or friends tend to suggest (in subtle or direct ways) that they think you should "do something with your life"? Do you make important decisions without considering the consequences? Are you at a point in your life where you need to decide your future, but you are unsure how to sort out the details?

By clarifying your reasons for pursuing a particular goal, you can make a commitment to complete it or choose to put your efforts somewhere else. For example, if you attend law school because someone else thinks it is the best thing for you to do, then you may start a difficult and expensive

13

undertaking without the motivation to complete it. Not only will you lack commitment, but you may be missing your true calling.

What Are the Real Reasons You Want to Do This?

"You can't push anyone up the ladder unless he is willing to climb himself."

—Andrew Carnegie (1835–1919), American steel industrialist

Looking carefully at the reasons behind pursuing a particular goal can help you decide if achieving it will truly satisfy your needs and wants. For example, let's say you are a sales manager who is considering a transfer to a different city because you are tired of your job. At first you follow the reasoning that "a change in scenery is as good as a vacation." After honestly examining the reasons behind your desire to move, however, you admit your real motivation. You are burned out by endless deadlines, bored to death writing sales reports, and tired of dealing with finicky clients. No matter where you choose to live, working in sales entails the same responsibilities. Therefore, moving to another city will probably not solve your problem. Once you reach this conclusion, considering a transfer to another department may be more beneficial for you. Or, you might think about retraining for a new career rather than merely changing your mailing address.

Consider the Consequences of Pursuing the Goal

"In soloing—as in other activities—it is easier to start something than it is to finish it."

—Amelia Earhart (1897–1937), American aviator
and first woman to make a solo transatlantic flight

Are you the spontaneous type who takes on major goals based purely on great expectations and unrealistic thinking? Making a snap decision about pursuing a goal can have far-reaching consequences. You can avoid rash decisions and missteps by answering certain questions before you go after a goal. Here is an example of how I used six questions to help me consider whether I should pursue a teaching career.

THE GOAL IN QUESTION: SHOULD I RETURN TO COLLEGE TO EARN A TEACHING DEGREE?

Question 1: *What are the pros and cons of pursuing this goal?*
Answer: The upside is that I will broaden my career opportunities if I earn a teaching degree. The downside is that I must give up playing in a band and teach even more guitar lessons to pay the tuition.

Question 2: *Is this the right time for this decision?*
Answer: The sooner I begin taking classes, the sooner I will finish the program and be able to get a full-time teaching

job. Besides, a local university is offering a nine-month certification program instead of the usual twelve-month program.

Question 3: *Are the risks of pursuing this goal worth the rewards?*
Answer: I'll be short on cash and may not get a full-time teaching job right away, but when the job opportunity arises, I'll be ready and certified.

Question 4: *Is this an impulsive decision?*
Answer: I have worked as a substitute teacher for two years and I enjoy working with kids in the classroom.

Question 5: *How will I benefit from my time and investment?*
Answer: It will take nine months of hard work and cost me some money, but I'll have a permanent teacher's certificate with which I can earn a good living. Besides, I like teaching music and working with kids, so I will enjoy this profession.

Question 6: *How will pursuing this goal affect my day-to-day living?*
Answer: I probably will not be able to socialize as much as I do now, and I'll really need to watch my expenses carefully. However, I can see my friends on the weekends and still teach guitar lessons in the evening to earn enough money to get by.

After I answered these six questions, I was confident that going back to school to earn a teacher's certificate was a good career decision—and I was right!

Make a List of Pros and Cons

Let's take a closer look at how to use a "pros and cons" list when considering whether to pursue a goal. My parents gave me some simple, yet excellent advice when it came to weighing the pros and cons of a goal. First divide a sheet of paper into two columns with the headings *pros* and *cons,* then start writing. When you see the benefits and disadvantages of a plan on paper, you can sort them out more easily. Then you can answer the question, "What have I got to gain? What have I got to lose?"

For example, I had been teaching elementary school for nearly six years and wanted to do something new. After my girlfriend at the time brought up the idea of moving to New York City, I decided to make a pros and cons list like this one:

Pros of Moving to New York

- ☆ Live in a center for the arts
- ☆ Find a more creative career
- ☆ Pursue music and publishing
- ☆ Increase my income
- ☆ Make new friends
- ☆ Fulfill dream of living there
- ☆ Study with professional musicians
- ☆ Live in a city of creative people

Cons of Moving to New York

- Lose contact with old friends
- Leave quiet house in the country
- Quit steady teaching position
- Lose a music-lesson business
- Find housing in a tough, big city
- Start a new business
- Lose steady income
- Upset my parents
- Higher cost of living
- Competition for music teachers
- Live in a more dangerous place

You'll get a chance to make your own pros and cons list in the exercise at the end of this chapter. As you make your list, keep in mind that taking on a major goal will not only affect you now, but also in the future. What you may consider a benefit today could turn out to be a drawback tomorrow. To identify the pros and cons of a decision, extend the consequences of your actions into the future as far as you can. For example, a college athlete may receive an offer to join a professional team during his junior year. While the benefits of earning a huge bonus sounds attractive now, an injury or poor performance (as well as forgoing a college degree) could eliminate a future opportunity to coach a college or professional team.

Visualize the Benefits of Achieving Your Goal

"It may be those who do the most, dream most."
—Stephen Leacock (1869–1944),
Canadian economist and humorist

Visualizing the benefits is another technique that can help you decide whether to pursue your goal. Use your imagination to visualize the future. Consider all the benefits for yourself and others when you set out and achieve the goal. Picture how your life and the lives of others will improve because of your achievement. To help you visualize the benefits of achieving your personal or professional goals, ask yourself these questions:

How do I expect my career to change when I achieve this professional goal?

How do I expect to benefit financially when I achieve this goal?

How do I expect my personal life to benefit when I achieve this goal?

How do I expect my family life to improve when I achieve this goal?

How do I expect to feel about myself when I achieve this goal?

How do I expect my social life to improve when I achieve this goal?

In what ways do I expect others to benefit when I achieve this goal?

Acknowledge the Downside

"I have made mistakes but I never made the mistake of claiming that I never made one."
—James Gordon Bennett (1841–1918),
American journalist who sent Stanley to Africa
to find Livingstone

While positive visualization helps you see the benefits of your endeavor, also think about what might happen if events do not unfold as you plan. Considering the risks of your actions and factoring them into the decision-making process is important. Then, if you think the risks are still worth the rewards, make a commitment to pursue your goal.

Ignoring or denying the drawbacks of any endeavor, whether it is starting a business, changing careers, or building a house, can lead to failure. Although thinking about difficult issues may be discouraging or painful, it is important to assess the potential costs of your pursuit and figure out who pays the price. Addressing the downside does not mean dwelling on the negative issues; it means acknowledging their existence and impact. Denying drawbacks to a pursuit does not make them go away; inevitably, they will rise up and bite you when you least expect it.

The following questions will help you uncover the possible negative consequences of pursuing the goal. Before you pursue a goal, ask yourself:

What hardships can my family and I expect to face?

What personal and financial sacrifices will my family and I need to make?

How might my personal relationships change for the worse?

How might my financial situation suffer?

How might this pursuit negatively affect my physical and emotional health (or anyone else's)?

How am I going to cope with the increased financial and emotional stress?

How long will I feel the financial and emotional stress?

Identify the *One* Negative Consequence That Outweighs All the Others

You can probably identify several areas where you and your family may need to make sacrifices. But can you zero in on *one* vulnerable point or negative consequence that, if left unaddressed, could lead to failure or an overwhelming hardship? To identify what could be a "fatal flaw" in your plan, ask yourself: Of all the possible negative repercussions of pursuing this goal, which *one* has the greatest potential to harm me or my family?

For example, I know a highly motivated entrepreneur who held two jobs and then spent every spare minute building his own small business. The biggest drawback to his ambitious goals was that his wife and children rarely saw him. When his family did see him, he was either tired, busy, or aggravated. Finally, after years of neglect, his wife divorced him and his family fell apart. The fatal flaw in this man's plan was that he put his business ambitions before his family's well-being and happiness.

If there is a fatal flaw in your plan that makes your pursuit impractical, then you may want to seriously consider abandoning or modifying the goal until certain circumstances change. On the other hand, if after honest reflection and discussion, everyone concerned can accept and deal with the greatest negative consequence, then your chances of overcoming this most threatening obstacle dramatically increase.

Trust Your Gut Instincts

"When making a decision of minor importance, I have always found it advantageous to consider all the pros and cons. In vital matters, however, such as the choice of a mate or a profession, the decision should come from the unconscious, from somewhere within ourselves."
—Sigmund Freud (1856–1939),
Austrian physician and father of modern psychiatry

No matter how carefully or objectively you compare and contrast the pros and cons of a particular decision, there comes a time when you need to listen to your intuition and ask yourself:

How do I really feel about this goal?

Is this what I really want in the long run?

Is it best for everyone concerned?

After carefully weighing the pros and cons of a goal, it's time to listen to your instincts. If your gut tells you it's the right decision, then make a commitment to pursue your dream—and give it everything you've got.

How to Deflect Outside Pressure When Pursuing a Goal

"Though thou hast never so many counselors, yet do not forsake the counsel of thy own soul."

—proverb

Whether they are your parents, friends, coworkers, or therapists, there are plenty of people who are happy to give you advice and tell you how to live your life. Of course, some of their advice may be good—even invaluable. But let's face it, what might be the right advice for one person could be wrong for you.

For example, the popular talk show host Rosie O'Donnell always wanted to be in show business, but not everyone thought she had what it takes to succeed. She explained her determination and attitude toward unsolicited advice this way: "When I was trying to be a movie star, people would tell me to quit, that I was too tough, too New York, too heavy. But I didn't listen to them. I thought, 'You're all idiots.'"

Some people may also pressure you into making a commitment that you really don't want or are not ready for. If you feel that a particular pursuit is not right for you or consistent with your goals and dreams, then assert yourself. You can say, "No, I don't want to do that. I appreciate your concern and suggestions, but that course of action is not right for me—at least not right now." Withstanding parental or peer pressure is difficult, especially if you have made few decisions of your own or rely heavily on others for moral or financial support. However, when you use the following assertive skills, you can stick up for yourself and not get pressured into decisions you may later regret.

DOS AND DON'TS FOR DEALING WITH A PUSHY PARENT

The following dos and don'ts will help you to remain poised and deflect the pressure exerted on you by a pushy parent or relative.

- **Do** remain silent for at least five seconds before you respond to a pushy relative's strongly worded suggestion. This implies that you have listened and are giving the comment some thought. (It also buys you a few moments to think about what he or she has said.)

- **Don't** immediately reject your pushy relative's advice. Chances are, some aspect of what he or she says may prove accurate or helpful. Say you'll think about it. (This may temporarily mollify the pushy parent, but not for long.)

Do ask the pushy person a "what if" question. For example, "What if I did become a legal secretary and hated it. What would you suggest I do then?" You can also bring up his or her past advice that was less than helpful. (This strategy may discourage heavy-handed suggestions, but don't count on it.)

Don't react to inflammatory statements or tactless remarks. These kinds of comments are calculated to make you lose your temper and appear out of control. When that happens, the parent will often say something like, "You're acting like a child," smugly implying that you're not mature enough to think for yourself. (Don't fall for this old trick.)

Do expect a pushy relative to be persistent. He or she will constantly "push your buttons," make you feel guilty, withhold approval, criticize unfairly, and dramatize the negative consequences for not following his or her advice. (Simply remain quiet. This will send the message that you have a mind of your own and you are going to use it.)

Don't be manipulated into doing something that your gut instinct says is wrong for you. (You won't be sorry. Just ask anyone suffering from a midlife crisis.)

Do keep your sense of humor and use it to defuse tense moments when you are about to lose your cool or feel the pressure to cave into the other person's demands. (If you lose your sense of humor, you've lost the battle.)

HERE'S WHAT YOU CAN SAY
TO A PUSHY PARENT

The following examples show how to assert your right to make your own decisions without the undue influence of a pushy parent.

Pushy parent: "I think you should go to trade school and become a dental assistant like your cousin. She makes good money and can always get a job. Besides, you might even marry your boss, and we could have a dentist in the family!"

Your response (Ignore the comment about marrying the boss): "You're right, Dad, finding a steady job is important, and I'm working on that. But, as for my career, I haven't decided what I want to do yet. I want to go to college, work at some different jobs, and see what I like and am good at before I choose a career."

Pushy parent: "We are the only ones in our group of friends who don't have any grandchildren. When I was your age, I already had three children, with a fourth on the way. Are you two having a problem in bed?"

Your response (ignore the sexual innuendo): "I know that you want grandchildren, but we both want to finish getting our college degrees before we have children. (Try a little joke to break the tension.) Do you want a few photos of our cats to show your friends?"

Pushy parent: "You still don't make a dime as a freelance artist, do you? Anyway, if you need to use a computer to draw, you can't be much of an artist. When are you going to grow up and get a real job? You should work with me in the family business. We really could use another salesman in the shoe department. You know, your old man could use a break after all these years. You can start Monday."

Your response (ignore the putdowns and the manipulation to make you feel guilty): "I appreciate the job offer, but the answer is no. Designing computer graphics may not be the easiest way for me to make a living, but I love what I'm doing. Sorry to let you down, but I'll pass on the job offer. If you're tired, Dad, take a vacation."

Pushy parent: "Moving into an apartment in the city is totally out of the question. With rents as high as they are, you'll never be able to make it without our help. And with all the crime, your mother will be so worried about you that she won't be able to sleep. At least you could have a little consideration for her! Why on earth would you want to live in that godforsaken place anyway?"

Your response (take deep breaths and stay cool during the barrage of negativity and fear): "I know that this is hard for you to understand, but making it on my own is important to me. Besides, I like the city, and an advertising agency has already offered me a job. Plus, I found a reasonably priced apartment in a safe neighborhood."

YOU HAVE THE RIGHT TO SAY NO

It takes guts to reject advice from a family member or someone you look up to. Here is what you can say:

To a relative trying to pressure you: "Joining the army might have been the best thing in the world for you, Uncle Bill, but that is not what I want to do. I prefer to work awhile, make some money, and then travel around and see the country."

To a friend trying to pressure you: "I agree your college has a winning football team and reputation for being a party school, but those things aren't really my cup of tea. I'm going to apply to a school that offers more of the kinds of courses that I'm interested in taking."

To an adult child trying to pressure you: "Son, I agree that living in a retirement community is a good idea for me, but I haven't seen an apartment that I like enough to buy. I know I'll find the right place for me if I'm patient and just keep looking."

Do What *You* Want to Do

In the end, your choice of pursuing long-term goals is up to you. Your decision may not be what others think is best for you or what they would choose for themselves. If your choice is contrary to someone else's opinion, remember the words of Henry David Thoreau: "If a man does not keep pace with his companions, perhaps it is because he hears the beat of a different drum."

LITTLE EXERCISES THAT GET BIG RESULTS

Number Two:
Making a Big Decision

> ### Problem-Solving Strategy:
> ### Making a Pros and Cons Chart
> *This strategy helps you zero in on the most*
> *important issues, establish your priorities,*
> *and simplify the decision-making process.*

What's the problem? Getting overwhelmed by details when considering a big decision is easy. One approach is to break the decision down into smaller, definable pieces to see how they affect you and other interested parties.

What to do: First, write a sentence defining the decision you want to make. Then fill in the pros and cons chart. Once you see how the benefits and disadvantages line up, making the big decision is really a matter of comparing several smaller key issues.

The big decision I am contemplating is:

_____

_____

_____

_____

The Pros Are: **The Cons Are:**

☆ _____   💣 _____

☆ _____   💣 _____

☆ _____   💣 _____

☆ _____   💣 _____

☆ _____   💣 _____

☆ _____   💣 _____

FOLLOW-UP

Now that you have listed the pros and cons, you can see which points are the most important. Also, some items in your chart may be assumptions while others are facts. Make your decision based on facts, not wishful (or fearful) thinking.

The two most important facts in the pros column are:

1. _____

2. _____

The two most important facts in the cons column are:

1. _____

2. _____

Based on the pros and cons, I have decided to:

_____

_____

_____

_____

_____

Little Things Checklist

Making a commitment to a big project can be scary, but once you do, you'll find it is a lot easier to achieve your goal. Here are more little things to think about before committing to a big goal.

✔ Take your time to choose the right goals for you.

✔ Experiment with different options before making a final commitment.

✔ Commit to a goal based on pros, cons, and your intuition.

✔ Listen to and consider the advice of knowledgeable people.

✔ Maintain the right to make your own decisions.

✔ Look at the facts from different perspectives.

✔ If necessary, gather more information before reaching a decision.

✔ Ask advice from others who have taken a similar path.

✔ When all is said and done, be courageous and pursue the goals that are right for you. After all, *it's your life!*

WHAT'S NEXT?

Now that you've figured out *why* you are pursuing a long-term goal, you're ready to go on to chapter three. Your next step is to define the obstacles that stand between you and your long-term goal.

3

Defining
Your Obstacles

"A problem is an opportunity in work clothes."
—Henry Kaiser (1882–1967), American industrialist

I ASKED A FRIEND who had moved from Seattle to New York how she overcame all the obstacles involved in making the big change. "After I made up my mind to move," she explained, "the first thing I did was write down everything I needed to do. Then I zeroed in on the biggest problem I needed to solve, which was to sell or rent my house. While I worked on that big problem, I also picked off the other smaller problems one at a time. Pretty soon, I was on my way to New York, ready to start a new life."

My friend achieved her goal by first defining her biggest obstacle, breaking it down into smaller, more manageable problems, and then attacking them head-on. At the same time, she accomplished all the other little things that needed to be done, too. You can use the same problem-solving skill to overcome the obstacles that stand between you and your goals. The following steps show you how.

Five Steps to Overcoming Obstacles

Step 1: Identify all your obstacles

Step 2: Categorize and prioritize major and minor obstacles

Step 3: Identify the "keystone" problem

Step 4: Chip away at the major and minor obstacles

Step 5: Develop several backup plans

Step One:
Identify All Your Obstacles

"A problem well stated is a problem half solved."
—Charles Kettering (1876–1958),
American inventor and engineer

Now that you know why you are pursuing a goal, what major problems or obstacles can you expect to encounter on your quest? How can you sort out the obstacles and focus on the most important issue? Which problems might be easier to solve and which one, if left unanswered, might cause you to fail? How can you anticipate, prepare for, and overcome these obstacles? How can you cope with the unexpected challenges that you are sure to face? Answering these questions will help you systematically overcome the problems that stand between you and your goal. One way to begin is to list any challenges, problems, hurdles, hindrances, and impediments you may encounter. For example, let's say you are considering moving your family to a new town. Without paying attention to the order, difficulty, or solutions to the problems, your random list of obstacles may look something like this:

List of Obstacles

❑ Break the news to the family

❑ Save money to pay for the move

❑ Find a new job

❑ Paint the new place before moving in

❑ Decide what to take or sell

❑ Pay deposit, and first and last month's rent

❑ Find a good school for the kids

❑ Find help moving the heavy items

❑ Find cheap packing supplies

❑ Advertise a moving sale

❑ Collect empty boxes

❑ Clean the apartment for deposit refund

❑ Find a new family doctor and dentist

❑ Get the kids registered for school

❑ Rent an affordable home in a good neighborhood that allows kids and pets

❑ Clean out rented storage space

❑ Fix the car's trailer hitch

❑ Help kids adapt to the move

❑ Find affordable day care

❑ Pack household items

Step Two:
Categorize and Prioritize
Major and Minor Obstacles

Whew! Looks overwhelming, doesn't it? There's no question that just the sheer volume of tasks, obstacles, and problems is enough to make you give up before you even begin. But don't get cold feet. Fortunately, not all obstacles are created equal. Although some problems require considerable persistence, skills, resources, and creativity to overcome, you can deal with others more easily. Categorizing specific problems into "Major Problems" and "Minor Obstacles" helps you identify how hard each will be to solve. Prioritizing the major problems helps you focus on the most important ones and tells you where to start. Maintaining an open list of minor obstacles allows you to pick off easier tasks as the opportunities arise. (You'll get a chance to categorize and prioritize the obstacles that stand between you and your goal in the exercise at the end of this chapter.) Building on the previous example, here is how you could categorize and prioritize the list of obstacles in Step One. You will notice that there are more minor obstacles than major obstacles connected with a typical long-term goal.

Major Problems
   (prioritized list)

1. Find a new job

2. Save money to pay for the move

3. Rent an affordable home, in a good neighborhood,

Minor Obstacles
   (random list)

❑ Break the news to the family

❑ Clean the new place before moving in

❑ Decide what to take or sell

that allows children and pets

4. Pay deposit, and first and last months' rent
5. Pay for moving expenses
6. Help kids adapt to the move
7. Find a good school for them
8. Find affordable day care
9. Pack stuff for the move

❏ Clean out the rented storage space

❏ Find help moving the heavy items

❏ Find cheap packing supplies

❏ Advertise a moving sale

❏ Clean the apartment for deposit refund

❏ Fix the car's trailer hitch

❏ Find a new family doctor and dentist

❏ Get the kids registered for school

❏ Find empty boxes

Step Three:
Identify the "Keystone" Problem

"Keystone: (1) the wedge-shaped piece at the crown of an arch that locks the other pieces in place. (2) something on which associated things depend for support."
— *Merriam Webster's Collegiate Dictionary, Tenth Edition*

Most major achievements result from overcoming many smaller hurdles. Usually, however, you must solve *one* critical obstacle or "keystone" problem before you can achieve your larger goal or purpose. In the example of moving to a new town, the keystone problem may be to find a new job. Without overcoming this problem, working through most of the other difficulties on your list may not be possible.

Keep in mind that although the keystone problem is critical to your success, it is not necessarily the most difficult obstacle to overcome. For example, if the company you presently work for has an office in the new town, then a job transfer may provide a simple solution to the keystone problem. At the same time, helping your children adapt to a new school and town may be more difficult.

Step Four:
Chip Away at the Major
and Minor Obstacles

"The only thing that separates successful people from the ones who aren't is the willingness to work very, very hard."
—Helen Gurley Brown (b. 1922),
author and editor-in-chief of *Cosmopolitan* magazine

Addressing the other priorities on your list is important. But in most cases, you will not have the luxury to devote all your time and resources to solving only your most difficult problems. The minor problems on your list need attention, too. Remember that if left unchecked, minor problems can turn into major stumbling blocks that are difficult to solve. You can quickly overcome many minor obstacles by taking care of the easier ones first. Keep chipping away at the little things you need to accomplish while you are hard at work on the more difficult problems. When you take this dual approach to dealing with obstacles, you will achieve your goals while saving yourself time and money.

Step Five:
Develop Several Backup Plans

"A thing long expected takes the form of the unexpected when at last it comes."
—Mark Twain, pseudonym of Samuel Langhorne Clemens (1835–1910),
American author and humorist

Trial attorney Edward Bennett Williams won many of his cases by applying the principle of "what can go wrong will go wrong." For example, when he questioned witnesses, he assumed that their testimony could turn up some unexpected facts that might undercut his case, so he anticipated what those facts might be and was ready to respond. Or, if the presiding judge denied his objections or curtailed his line of inquiry, he always armed himself with another question or strategy. By doing his homework and preparing for the worst possible outcomes, Williams was victorious in court most of the time.

Facing unexpected drawbacks, crises, or sudden changes makes dealing with tough obstacles even more difficult. Sure, a crystal ball would be helpful when pursuing big goals, but anticipating every possible hardship or roadblock is impossible. However, you can prepare for surprises that stretch your time, resources, and patience. By being flexible and able to respond quickly, you can get back on track with as little downtime as possible. One of the greatest threats to your success is not preparing for what can go wrong. Here are some simple yet effective ways to prepare for the unexpected.

◆ Take a what-can-go-wrong-*will*-go-wrong approach to uncover potential obstacles. Don't drive yourself crazy, but look realistically at the probability of things not always going in your favor.

◆ To elicit alternative responses and strategies, ask yourself, "If Plan A fails, what will be my next step?"

◆ Always prepare backup plans for dealing with obstacles if your first option or plan fails.

◆ Create a cash reserve exclusively for unexpected problems. Buying your way out of a difficult situation is sometimes the best solution.

◆ When planning, allot extra time and resources to deal with unexpected problems. If you don't use the time sooner, you'll probably need it later.

◆ Don't wait for the unexpected to happen before you test your ability to react in a crisis. Occasionally ask yourself, "If the worst thing happens today, tomorrow I would . . ."

Dealing with Obstacles
Requires a Positive Attitude

"No matter how cynical you become, it's never enough to keep up."
—Lily Tomlin (b. 1939),
American actress and comedian

You've probably heard the expression, "attitude is everything." Well, it's true when it comes to overcoming obstacles and achieving your goals. A positive, can-do attitude helps you take advantage of opportunities. On the other hand, a negative attitude can be a greater obstacle than any technical or logistical problem separating you from your goal. If you find yourself blaming others for your failures, or if you expect someone else to solve your problems, then your attitude may be your biggest obstacle. No matter how talented, intelligent, or deserving you are, if you have an attitude problem, your ship of dreams will sink faster than the *Titanic.* A negative attitude can sap your confidence and desire to solve even the minor challenges you face.

Take an attitude check. Do you find yourself saying any of the statements in the "Can't Do" column? If so, change them into "Can Do" statements.

"Can't Do" Attitude	**"Can Do" Attitude**
"This is inconvenient."	"I'll do it now."
"I think this idea is stupid."	"I'll see what happens."
"I can't do this."	"I'll do the best I can."
"I don't know what to do."	"I can start here."
"This will never work."	"I've got a backup plan."
"I don't know how."	"Someone can teach me how."
"I'll never finish."	"I'm well on my way."

Solving Problems Leads to Success, Opportunity, and Confidence

"I have learned that success is to be measured not so much by the position that one has reached in life as by the obstacles which one has overcome while trying to succeed."
—Booker T. Washington (1856–1915), American educator

You will be amazed at what you can accomplish when you focus your efforts on solving the specific and well-defined obstacles that stand between you and your goal. Not only will you find solutions to your problems more quickly, but you'll become more confident and proficient in the process. J. C. Penney, the founder of the vast department store enterprise, put it this way: "I am grateful for all my problems. After each one was overcome, I became stronger and more able to meet those that were still to come. I grew in all my difficulties."

LITTLE EXERCISES THAT GET BIG RESULTS

Number Three:
Hey Buddy,
What's Your Problem?

Problem-Solving Strategy:
Making a List of Obstacles

This strategy helps you sort, classify, and identify
key problems so that you can focus on solving
the ones most crucial to your success.

What's the problem? Problems, problems! To accomplish your goals you must deal with dozens or hundreds of tasks, details, and obstacles. Ask yourself: Which *one* problem is more important than all the rest?

What to do: The objective of this exercise is to classify obstacles based on their difficulty and then set your priorities. Write each problem, challenge, obstacle, and task related to your goal under the headings "Major Obstacles" or "Minor Obstacles." Set the priorities for your major obstacles only.

My goal:

_____

_____

_____

Major Obstacles
   (prioritized list)

Minor Obstacles
   (random list)

1. _____
2. _____
3. _____
4. _____
5. _____
6. _____
7. _____
8. _____

❑ _____
❑ _____
❑ _____
❑ _____
❑ _____
❑ _____
❑ _____
❑ _____
❑ _____
❑ _____
❑ _____
❑ _____
❑ _____

FOLLOW-UP

Now that you have listed your major and minor obstacles, identify your keystone problem and write a few possible solutions. Remember that a keystone problem is the *one* problem that you must overcome to achieve your goal.

My goal:

_____

_____

_____

_____

_____

_____

Keystone problem:

_____

_____

_____

_____

Plan A:

_____

_____

_____

_____

Plan B: (Backup)

_____

_____

_____

_____

Plan C: (Backup)

_____

_____

_____

_____

Little Things Checklist

Dealing with details and solving problems are tall orders, but that's what it is going to take to achieve your dreams. Do these additional little things to help yourself identify and overcome the obstacles that stand between you and your goal.

- ✔ See problems and obstacles as signposts on the way to your goal.

- ✔ Deal with little problems before they become big ones.

- ✔ Focus most of your efforts on the keystone problem.

- ✔ Ask people for help or ideas if you can't find a solution on your own.

- ✔ Look for alternative ways to solve problems and get over obstacles.

- ✔ Approach big problems in small doses so you don't get overwhelmed.

- ✔ Define the obstacles clearly before applying solutions.

- ✔ Ask the right questions to get the right solutions.

- ✔ Observe how others approach and solve problems like yours.

- ✔ Go over, under, around, or through the obstacles that you face.

WHAT'S NEXT?

Now that you have learned how to categorize the obstacles that stand between you and your goal, you're ready to go on to chapter four. Your next step is to face the fear and do it anyway.

4

Facing the Fear of
Falling Flat on Your Face

"All adventures, especially into new territory, are scary."
—Sally Ride (b. 1951),

first American woman astronaut to fly in space

I REMEMBER THE DAY I decided to quit my job teaching in an elementary school, sell my house near Vancouver, British Columbia, and move to New York City. I enjoyed teaching, but I was getting bored with the routine and wanted to explore a more creative career in music and educational publishing. When I told my parents about my plans, they flipped. Never mind that I was thirty-two years old and already living 1,500 miles from their home. My father started: "You're doing *what?* You're going to throw away everything you've worked for? The last thing in the world New York needs is another guitar teacher." But my mother went directly for the jugular: "If I only live ten more years and I see you once a year, I'll only see you ten more times. How could you do this to me?"

I got nervous and had second thoughts. I asked myself repeatedly, "Are they right? Am I making a big mistake? Is there something about Mother's health that I didn't know about? Am I just fooling myself, thinking I can make it in the toughest city in the world?"

Questions and negative comments like these nearly derailed my dream of finding a new career in New York. However, after thinking about the situation, I realized that my parents were only expressing their fears for my future. I, too, was wondering whether I would make it in the Big Apple, but I decided to give myself a year and see what would happen. Although I was willing to take a major risk to achieve my dream of a more exciting career, my parents saw my actions as only a reckless gamble. If I had let it, their fear could have become my fear and self-doubt, too.

Confronting Your Self-Doubts

"Our doubts are our traitors, and make us lose the good we oft might win, by fearing to attempt."
—William Shakespeare (1564–1616), English dramatist and poet

Even the great Italian opera singer Enrico Caruso had to fight self-doubt. As he waited backstage before an opening night performance, stagehands heard him whispering to himself, "Get out of my way! Get out! Get out!" After the opera, a curious worker asked Caruso about his whispering. The great tenor explained, "I felt within the big me that wants to sing and knows it can, but it was being stifled by the little me that gets afraid and says 'I can't.' I was simply ordering the little me out of my body."

Another example of the notion of fear comes from Louis, Lord Mountbatten, the great naval commander and great-grandson of Queen Victoria. As a young child, Mountbatten was afraid to sleep in a dark room. "It isn't the dark," he said to his father. "There are wolves up there." Mountbatten's father tried to convince his son that there were no wolves in the house and that his bedroom was completely safe. The boy, however, was not persuaded. He said, "I daresay there aren't," he stated confidently, "but I think there are."

Like Enrico Caruso and Lord Mountbatten, you too may have secret or nameless fears. How you deal with your reservations, anxieties, and insecurities can make the difference between success and failure as you seek to fulfill your ambitions. By acknowledging and facing your fears, you increase your chances of overcoming self-doubt and accomplishing your goals.

Dealing with Other People's Fears

"The first and great commandment is: Don't let them scare you."
—Elmer Davis (1890–1958),
American writer and radio news commentator

Just when you are about to make that big decision, don't be surprised when some well-meaning friends or family members bombard you with all kinds of reasons not to pursue your goal. If you are not ready to counter their negativity, they can undermine your confidence and motivation.

Here is how to assertively handle other people's fear and negativity. First, agree with some element in their statement by repeating or paraphrasing the critical words. Then repeat your intention to stick to your decision. By following this assertive strategy, you'll wear down the critical person, and increase your confidence and motivation to succeed. Here are some typical fearful comments and assertive ways to respond.

Fearful comment: "You're biting off way more than you can chew."

Assertive response: "You may be right that I am taking on a big challenge, but I'm going to give it my best shot and see what happens."

Fearful comment: "Do you know what kind of competition you'll be up against? People with a lot more talent than you don't make it. What makes you think you can do it?"

Assertive response: "I'm sure the competition is tough, but I'm determined to try my best and see what happens."

Fearful comment: "You'll probably fall flat on your face! What will you do then?"

Assertive response: "You may be right. I might fall flat on my face. If that happens, I'll pick myself up and begin again. I may not succeed, but I won't know if I can make it if I don't try."

Fearful comment: "I just don't understand why you're risking everything you've worked so hard for. Have you lost your mind?"

Assertive response: "I agree that I'm taking a big risk, and I know that might be hard for you to understand. But I want to accomplish more than I am doing now, and if that means taking a risk, then so be it."

Fearful comment: "Isn't there anything I can say to talk you out of this ridiculous idea? I don't want to see you get hurt."

Assertive response: "Maybe this idea is ridiculous, and I appreciate your concern for me. I'd be really happy if you were behind me, but I'm going to stick to my decision and give this my best shot—with or without your support."

Keep the Fear of Failure in Perspective

"You must do the thing you think you cannot do."
—Eleanor Roosevelt (1884–1962),
American diplomat and humanitarian

When your fears of what can go wrong go unchecked, they can undermine your confidence and paralyze your efforts. A more productive way of dealing with fear is to think realistically, not catastrophically about failing. If you consider a few alternate strategies before you attempt to make a change, then your fears will not prevent you from taking the risks necessary to succeed.

For instance, what would I do if I "crashed and burned" in New York City? I figured that the worst thing that could happen was that I would have to find another job teaching school somewhere in the area. By identifying my "worst case" scenario and by having an acceptable alternative plan, I felt more confident about making the big decision to move.

Maybe my friends and family were right when they told me I was crazy to give up a good job and "throw away" everything I had worked for. Perhaps I had seen too many movies or read too many books about people who followed their dreams and succeeded. There was no question about it that the odds were in favor of my falling flat on my face in an unfamiliar and unforgiving city. Ultimately, however, I concluded that my life would go on, even if I did fail. What I could not accept was the idea of never knowing if I would succeed or fail because I was afraid to try. Therefore, I decided to take the risk, move to New York City, and give my dream the best shot I could. So, that's what I did.

Harness the Fear
and Make It Work for You

"I work on fear. I have not overcome a certain insecurity, and God help me, I hope I never lose it, or I'll be lousy."
  —Jack Lemmon (b. 1925),
  American film and stage actor

Overcoming fear takes courage. Call it chutzpah, audacity, nerve, daring, guts, brazenness, or tenacity. Courage is harnessing fear and making it work for you. It is mental and moral strength to venture out or persevere in spite of the risk of failure. You have calculated the risks to the best of your ability. Now it is time for action. So, take a deep breath and say to yourself in a strong, loud voice, "I'm going to take the plunge and see what happens. I may succeed. I may fail. But at least I'll have the personal satisfaction of knowing that I went after what I wanted. Whatever happens, I know that I'm a survivor."

LITTLE EXERCISES THAT GET BIG RESULTS
Number Four:
Focusing on Your Success

Problem-Solving Strategy:
Seeing Yourself Successful

This strategy employs the same visualization techniques
that many athletes and performers use to help them
conquer fears and produce winning results.
By visualizing what is possible, you can
overcome real and self-imposed barriers.

What's the problem? When fears start to creep into your mind, they can stop you from taking risks or impede your rate of progress toward your goal. You can eliminate some of the insidious damage that fear can wreak on your dreams by replacing fearful images with successful ones.

What to do: The objective of this exercise is to develop images of yourself succeeding in your goal. Find a quiet place where you can relax and remain undisturbed. Use the following questions to help you see yourself as successful. Imagine as many details as you can. The pictures you create are up to you, so pull out all the stops and have fun!

1. My specific long-term goal is to: _____
    _____

2. The situation in which I see myself achieving this
    goal: _____

3. The specific actions I see myself engaged in are: _____
    _____

4. The people I see with me in this situation include: ____
    _____

5. The most amazing things that I see happening in this
    situation are: _____

FOLLOW-UP

Rational and irrational fears can plague even the most confident high achievers. When this happens to you, take a separate sheet of paper and list all the fears you have about
pursuing your dream goal. Most people are afraid of rejection,
criticism, and failure. Also include what some people might
say to you if you fail, as well as some catastrophic events that
could derail your plan.

After you have made your lists, read the fears aloud. Then
take your list of fears, tear it into little pieces, and throw
them into the trash. When you think of other fears, write
them down on a new sheet of paper. Read them aloud, rip up
the paper, and throw it away. Repeat this step as often as
necessary, and soon those old fears that have tried to undermine your efforts in the past won't even bother rearing their
ugly heads.

Little Things Checklist

Dealing with the fear of failure and rejection is an ongoing process. Here are some additional tips to help you overcome misgivings and doubts about pursuing your dreams.

✔ When fears creep in and undercut your confidence, knock them out of your head by repeating "I-can-do-it" messages to yourself.

✔ Know the difference between realistic and irrational fears.

✔ Don't let other people's fear and negativity contaminate your desire for success.

✔ Be ready to face your fears and pursue your dreams.

✔ Think about how you have overcome past fears and apply the lessons you learned to your new situation and endeavor.

✔ Stay calm and keep in control when irrational fears threaten your progress.

✔ Don't let your fears prevent you from using all your available resources to succeed.

✔ Continue to face new fears and you will build your confidence and ability to succeed.

WHAT YOU'VE LEARNED IN STEP ONE

Seeing where you want to be in the future is the first step in your journey toward success. You now see that you can decide what you want to happen in your life, instead of waiting for someone or something to make your dreams become a reality. Once you can see the "big picture," you can identify your motivation. Then you can begin the process of defining your obstacles. Now you understand that not all obstacles are equally difficult or require the same kind of attention. After learning how to set your priorities, you now know how to deal with the fears that can undermine your confidence and ability to succeed in your endeavors.

WHAT'S NEXT?

Now you are ready to go on to "Step Two, Plan Your Action" and chapter five. Your next step is to map out the midterm goals that will lead you to the realization of your dreams.

Step Two

PLAN YOUR ACTIONS

"Our plans miscarry because they have no aim. When a man does not know what harbor he is making for, no wind is the right wind."

—Lucius Annaeus Seneca (c. 4 B.C.–A.D. 65),
Roman statesman and philosopher

5

Mapping Out Your Big Steps

"He who aims for the moon may hit the top of the tree; he who aims at the top of the tree is unlikely to get off the ground."

—proverb

I N THE HOT summer of 1958 my mother, father, sister, and I drove across California's blistering Mojave desert on our way to the High Sierra Mountains. I was thirsty, so I asked my parents when we would stop and get something to drink. My father told me to read the signs along the road and I would have the answer. Every mile or so along the roadway billboards advertised frosty drinks and displayed the number of miles to the next dusty town. My desire for a cool root beer float grew stronger with every passing billboard.

Make Your Own Billboards for Your Midterm Goals

"It is good to have an end to journey toward; but it is the journey that matters, in the end."

—Ursula K. LeGuin (b. 1929), American writer

Billboards that show you are traveling in the right direction and moving closer to your destination make any long journey seem shorter and easier. As you move toward a long-term goal, you can set up your own billboards in the form of midterm goals. These midterm goals help you achieve your dreams by allowing you to:

◆ Keep on the right road

◆ Measure your progress

◆ Anticipate future obstacles

◆ Make necessary corrections

◆ Build momentum as you work through a project

◆ Increase confidence that you will achieve the goal

Florence Chadwich, the first woman to swim the English Channel, learned the hard way about the importance of setting midterm goals. In 1952, after years of grueling training, her big day arrived; she dove into the waters off the coast of France and started swimming for the English shoreline. Florence toiled hour after hour while her mother and fans cheered her on from small boats accompanying her across the water. As she neared the English coastline, a thick fog descended onto the channel, and the cold, choppy waters became even more difficult to pass through. Exhausted and unaware that she was only a few hundred yards from England, Florence asked her friends to help her from the water.

When Florence learned how close she had come to reaching the English coast, she was bitterly disappointed. Determined to try again, she devised a plan to overcome the obstacle of not knowing her location if the fog rolled into the channel again. She created mental images of the English coastline from various points in the channel. These images would serve as midterm goals, or billboards, and tell her approximately how much farther she had to swim before reaching the shore. After regaining her strength and training again for months, Florence repeated her attempt to swim the channel. With each stroke, she could see the English coast getting closer. Then the inevitable fog set in and the waters became choppy. This time, however, she was ready. By visualizing her position in the channel as she continued to swim through the fog, she knew that she was on course. With the help of her mental billboards, and a great deal of perseverance, Florence Chadwich became the first woman to swim the English Channel.

How Do You Create Your Own Billboards?

"Everything should be made as simple as possible, but not one bit simpler."

—Albert Einstein (1879–1955),
German-born American physicist

Like billboards on the edge of a road, your midterm goals must be clearly visible so you can follow them to that big payoff. Follow these four steps to create you own midterm goals, or billboards, and *L-E-A-P* into action:

L-E-A-P into Action

Midterm goals are the billboards that guide you to your destination. L-E-A-P into action, and you will begin your journey.

L = List as many midterm goals as you can think of

E = Evaluate the midterm goals

A = Ascertain missing midterm goals

P = Prioritize midterm goals

L = LIST AS MANY MIDTERM GOALS AS YOU CAN THINK OF

List as many midterm goals as you can possibly think of that may help you accomplish your long-term goal. Depending on your endeavor, the number of midterm goals you identify will vary. Don't worry about evaluating and sequencing them right now. You can do that later.

For example, let's say that you want to remodel your kitchen. You've done your research and know that this can be a long and costly process, so you need to break this big job down into smaller, more manageable units. Remember that you may not think of the most important steps first or in the right order. You can begin this process by asking yourself:

What midterm goals do I need to accomplish to complete the project?

For example, here are some possible midterm goals (in no particular order) for remodeling a kitchen:

❑ Research commonly used kitchen layouts

❑ Decide the extent of the renovation

❑ Secure financing to pay for the remodeling

❑ Make a detailed budget and schedule for the job

❑ Hire an architect to draw a set of plans

❑ Make a layout of the appliances, shelves, and cabinets

❑ Choose the materials and fixtures

❑ Hire the professionals to do the work

❑ Learn a computer software program to design kitchen layout

❑ Pick out and purchase the flooring, countertops, cabinets, appliances, and other fixtures

❑ Create a work schedule with the electrician, plumber, and other workers

❑ Plan alternative ways to prepare meals during the renovation

❑ Rearrange your work schedule so you can be home while the work is taking place

❑ Get references and see the work of the contractors before you agree to use them

E = EVALUATE THE MIDTERM GOALS

Once you have written as many midterm goals as you can think of, you will need to evaluate each and its role in achieving your long-term goal. Identifying only the most critical midterm goals is important. This is necessary because your list will probably include many goals, tasks, and steps of varying degrees of difficulty. If you were to give all these midterm goals equal weight, you might feel overwhelmed and give up.

Again, you can use the roadside billboard as a model. Each midterm goal expresses one primary obstacle and acts as a milestone on the way to your destination. You will address the other, less important tasks and smaller steps on your list later in the process. You can evaluate a midterm goal by asking yourself questions like these:

Is achieving my long-term goal contingent upon this midterm goal?

For example, the midterm goal of carefully planning the exact location of every appliance and cabinet avoids costly and time-consuming changes later on.

How does this midterm goal help me achieve my long-term goal?

For example, hiring professionals instead of doing all the work myself will probably save money and time in the end.

Will this midterm goal keep me on track or take my efforts in a new direction that diverts my attention from my original long-term goal?

For example, the benefits of learning a computer software program to design the kitchen may not be worth the time and effort that you have to invest in it.

A = ASCERTAIN MISSING MIDTERM GOALS

Have you ever woken up in the middle of the night and realized that you have forgotten something important? When I plan and execute a project, I'm always on the lookout for what I call "the grand omission." After I have listed every midterm goal I can think of, I look at my list again. I often realize that I have overlooked at least one more important midterm goal— usually the one that was most obvious. The cliché about not being able to see the woods for the trees applies here. When you are planning your big steps toward a long-term goal, take some extra time to consider which midterm goals you may have forgotten. Chances are, if you look hard enough, you'll probably find that you left an important midterm goal off your list.

Take for example the failed food product, "Wine & Dine," a prepackaged dinner that came with a small bottle of wine— that is, wine for cooking, not drinking. One midterm goal the manufacturer forgot was to test-market its package design. The problem became evident despite the words "Not for Beverage Use" and a picture of the wine being poured over the food as it was being cooked. Many consumers drank the salty and spicy wine mixture. Perhaps if the manufacturer had not overlooked the midterm goal of testing the package on a group of consumers first, before sending its product out into the marketplace, this clever idea for home gourmet cooking might have been a tasteful success.

P = PRIORITIZE MIDTERM GOALS

When Charles M. Schwab was president of Bethlehem Steel, he spent the last few minutes of each day deciding which tasks he would deal with first thing the next morning. He always prioritized the tasks and completed them in order until he had finished the list. Schwab remarked, "This is the most practical lesson I've ever learned." Then he illustrated his point with an anecdote. "I had put off a phone call for nine months, so I decided to list it as my number-one task on my next day's agenda. That call netted us a two-million-dollar order."

How do you prioritize your midterm goals? It's easy if you ask yourself questions like these:

What are the six most important midterm goals?

What midterm goal must come first?

What is the specific objective of this midterm goal?

How does it relate to other my other midterm goals?

What must I accomplish before I can achieve this midterm goal?

What other midterm goal is contingent upon this midterm goal?

The following page shows how to use billboards to prioritize six critical midterm goals for remodeling a kitchen. Once you have set the priorities of the six most important midterm goals, you can address the other midterm goals in their appropriate sequence.

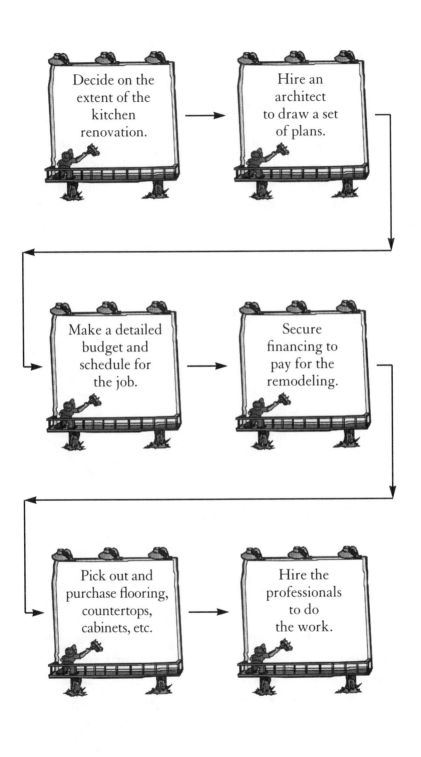

Decide on the extent of the kitchen renovation.

Hire an architect to draw a set of plans.

Make a detailed budget and schedule for the job.

Secure financing to pay for the remodeling.

Pick out and purchase flooring, countertops, cabinets, etc.

Hire the professionals to do the work.

Reward Yourself When You Achieve Your Midterm Goals

Identifying a simple yet meaningful reward for yourself each time you achieve a midterm goal is important. The cost of the reward is not as important as receiving it close to the time you completed your midterm goal. This strategy of positive reinforcement makes you feel good about your efforts and motivates you to continue working on the other midterm goals on your list.

Passing Your Own Billboards Means Making Progress

"I do the very best I know how—the very best I can; and I mean to keep doing so until the end."
—Abraham Lincoln (1809–1865),
sixteenth president of the United States

High achievers know the value of midterm goals. First, these interim goals provide a map and measuring stick for your progress. As you pass each billboard, you have the opportunity to make the needed adjustments or course corrections. Perhaps you discover something that makes your next task easier, or you come up with a possible solution to an obstacle that you are soon to encounter. Your billboards will help you figure out which aspects of your plan work and which ones need revising. As a result, you can keep tweaking the midterm goals until they work just right. Plus, knowing that you are on course and making progress on your midterm goals sustains your efforts to achieve your long-term goal.

LITTLE EXERCISES THAT GET BIG RESULTS

Number Five:
Creating Your Billboards
to Success

Problem-Solving Strategy:
Developing a
Midterm Goals Flowchart

*This strategy helps you establish the sequence
of midterm goals from the beginning to the end
of your long-term goal.*

What's the problem? Many people give up on achieving their dreams because they do not clearly identify all the necessary midterm goals in the process. Mapping out your midterm goals will keep you on course and allow you to prepare for and overcome future obstacles.

What to do: The objective of this exercise is to identify and prioritize the six most important midterm goals that lead to your dream. Then write a few words on each billboard to describe each major obstacle you need to overcome.

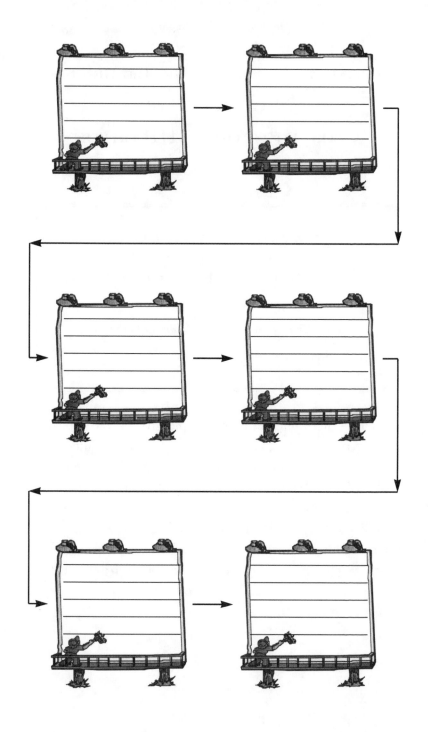

FOLLOW-UP

You now have a plan with your six most important midterm goals. The next step is to identify the "keystone" problem (see chapter three) for each midterm goal. Then consider possible ways to solve each problem. This strategy helps you anticipate the tough patches that lay ahead and gives you time to think about and prepare potential solutions.

Midterm goal 1: _____

Keystone problem: _____

_____

Possible solution:_____

_____

_____

Midterm goal 2: _____

Keystone problem: _____

_____

Possible solution: _____

_____

_____

Midterm goal 3: _____

Keystone problem: _____

_____

_____

Possible solution:_____

_____

_____

_____

_____

Midterm goal 4: _____

Keystone problem: _____

_____

_____

Possible solution:_____

_____

_____

_____

_____

Midterm goal 5: _____

Keystone problem: _____

_____

_____

Possible solution: _____

_____

_____

_____

Midterm goal 6: _____

Keystone problem: _____

_____

_____

Possible solution: _____

_____

_____

_____

_____

Little Things Checklist

Although identifying and prioritizing midterm goals takes time and consideration, it is well worth the effort. Here are some additional tips to help you zero in on the most important tasks that lead to your long-term goals.

- ✔ Avoid automatic yes or no answers when considering your midterm goals.

- ✔ Keep thinking of new ways to get past the tough obstacles.

- ✔ Redefine vague midterm goals so you know exactly what you want to achieve.

- ✔ Write down your midterm goals and post them where you can see them each day.

- ✔ Give yourself reasonable deadlines for accomplishing your midterm goals.

- ✔ After completing one midterm goal, reward yourself. Then immediately attack your next midterm goal.

WHAT'S NEXT?

Now that you have defined the most important midterm goals that lead to your dream, you can go on to chapter six. Your next step is to organize all those little details.

6

Organizing Your Little Steps

*"The person who makes a success of living is the one who sees his goal
steadily and aims for it unswervingly."*
— Cecil B. DeMille (1881–1959),
American film producer and director

I HAD TO ACCOMPLISH several midterm goals before I
could achieve my dream of moving to New York City.
After I sold my house, I needed to get rid of most of my
household items and scrape together as much cash as possible,
so I decided to have a moving sale. Getting organized for a
moving sale took considerable time and energy, but it was
worth it. I achieved my midterm goal and moved one big step
closer to fulfilling my dream.

Your ability to focus on critical details is the key to accomplishing your midterm goals and to realizing your big dreams.
In chapter five you learned how to break down a long-term
goal into several key midterm goals. Now you need to divide
each midterm goal into small, manageable steps so they are
easy to execute.

Henry Ford mass-produced the automobile with this strategy: Break down one big job into many little steps. If you want to accomplish your midterm and long-term goals, the strategy of focusing on little steps can help you in several ways. First, it allows you to focus on simpler steps or problems, one at a time. By zeroing in on the small steps that lead to midterm goals, you can establish a systematic approach or "order of operations" that allows for adjustments and increases your efficiency. Finally, tackling many small, clearly defined tasks keeps you from becoming overwhelmed by the sheer magnitude of a challenging goal.

Break a Midterm Goal into a Series of Organized Little Steps

"Great engines turn on small pivots."
—proverb

If you are eager to pursue a midterm goal, then you probably have little trouble diving in and executing the first few steps. However, you may stumble on third, fourth, or subsequent steps. On the other hand, if you are a reluctant starter, the first few steps may be so intimidating that you hesitate to begin at all. The following steps help the eager and reluctant starter focus on the little steps that lead to achieving midterm goals.

STEP ONE:
WHAT IS THE SPECIFIC PURPOSE
OF THE MIDTERM GOAL?

"The man who starts out going nowhere, generally gets there."
—Dale Carnegie (1888–1955),
author and lecturer on public speaking and self-esteem

Breaking Down a Midterm Goal into Little Steps

Step 1: What is the specific purpose of the midterm goal?

Step 2: What little steps do I need to take to achieve the midterm goal?

Step 3: In what order do I execute the steps?

Step 4: Approximately how long will it take me to complete each step?

Specifically define the purpose of the midterm goal before you break it down into smaller steps. If your purpose is vague, then the steps you identify may be too general or incomplete to be helpful. For example, when I decided to have a moving sale, I had a clearly defined midterm goal. The specific purpose of this sale was to empty my house of furniture and other unwanted items and make some money so I could buy new household necessities when I got to New York.

Whatever your midterm goal happens to be, just make sure you know what specific purpose it is supposed to serve. If you are unclear as to the purpose of the midterm goal, then consider going back and redefining it. Once you have clearly defined the purpose of the midterm goal, go on to Step Two.

STEP TWO:
WHAT LITTLE STEPS DO I NEED TO TAKE TO ACHIEVE THE MIDTERM GOAL?

Now is the time to focus on all the little things you need to do to accomplish a specific midterm goal. List every step you can think of, from the easiest to the most difficult, including the most obvious. Don't worry if you list the items in order, just get them down on paper. For example, I needed to take the following little steps to have a successful moving sale:

- ❑ Clean out all the closets
- ❑ Decide what goes in the sale
- ❑ Make signs for the sale
- ❑ Put an advertisement in the paper
- ❑ Get some help from a friend
- ❑ Take unsold items to a thrift store
- ❑ Put signs up in the neighborhood
- ❑ Clean the garage
- ❑ Set up display tables
- ❑ Put price tags on the items
- ❑ Organize the merchandise
- ❑ Collect empty boxes

Again, the details will vary depending on your midterm goal, but the key to this step is writing down *all* the little things you can think of. After getting a good start on this list (you'll keep adding more things as you think of them), go on to Step Three.

STEP THREE:
IN WHAT ORDER DO I EXECUTE THE STEPS?

"Logic is the art of going wrong with confidence."
—Joseph Wood Krutch (1893–1970),
American critic and naturalist

Now that you know all the steps that lead to a specific midterm goal, how do you figure out the order in which to do them? One way is to create a flowchart that shows each step in sequence. Since there is usually more than one way to achieve a midterm goal, you can use a combination of logical thinking, trial and error, and experience to create your flowchart. The following page shows a six-step flowchart that I used to organize my moving sale. You'll have a chance to complete your own six-step flowchart in the exercise at the end of this chapter.

By creating a flowchart, you can clearly see the order of all the little steps you need to take to achieve your midterm goal. You don't need a fancy computer program to make a useful flowchart: Pencil and paper will do just fine. Writing your little steps helps you focus on the details while seeing how they help you achieve your midterm goal. You can see which steps you have completed and which ones remain to be done. You can identify any steps you have overlooked and eliminate those that are unnecessary. The benefit of the flowchart is that you can make your mistakes on paper and correct them before putting your plan into action.

It will take only a few extra minutes to organize the little steps on a flowchart, but you will eliminate errors, save time, and avoid wasting valuable resources. Once you have created a flowchart of all the little steps you need to complete your midterm goal, then go on to Step Four.

STEP FOUR:
APPROXIMATELY HOW LONG
WILL IT TAKE ME TO COMPLETE EACH STEP?

The answer to this question varies from step to step. You can begin by identifying which small steps will probably

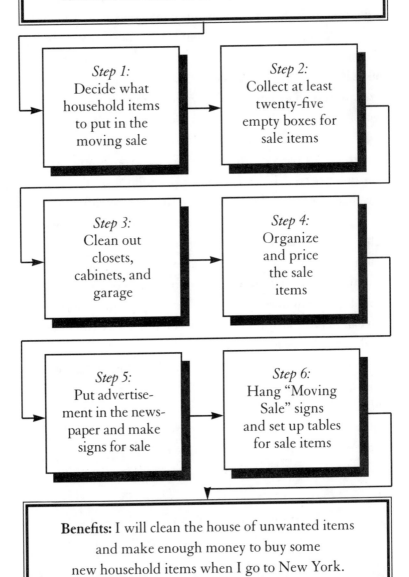

Midterm goal: Have a moving sale to get rid of my furniture and other unwanted household items.

Step 1:
Decide what household items to put in the moving sale

Step 2:
Collect at least twenty-five empty boxes for sale items

Step 3:
Clean out closets, cabinets, and garage

Step 4:
Organize and price the sale items

Step 5:
Put advertisement in the newspaper and make signs for sale

Step 6:
Hang "Moving Sale" signs and set up tables for sale items

Benefits: I will clean the house of unwanted items and make enough money to buy some new household items when I go to New York.

take the most time. Then you can make a rough guess how long it will take to achieve the midterm goal. Most estimates do not need to be down to the minute. However, if you accurately estimate how long it will take you to complete the midterm goal, then you can allot enough time for all the steps. When you make your estimate, allow extra time for dealing with potential trouble spots or unexpected problems. This will give you added leeway to complete your midterm goal. (Chapter thirteen, "Setting and Meeting Your Own Deadlines" focuses specifically on this frequent problem.)

You can avoid frustration by accurately estimating how long it will take you to finish a little step. For example, I had an unassembled fancy barbecue grill with a domed cover, retractable sides, and many other gizmos that I wanted to include in my moving sale. Seeing the words "No tools required—easy to assemble" printed on the box, I assumed that I could put the contraption together in about an hour. That estimate was purely wishful thinking! After forty-five minutes of trying to interpret two pages of incomprehensible instructions, I had numerous nuts, bolts, and a dozen other parts strewn all over the ground. Since the assembly was taking far longer than I anticipated, I finally gave up, put the darn thing back in the box, and sold it "as is."

This story has two lessons: First, if you can accurately estimate how long a task will take to complete, you can save yourself a good deal of frustration. Second, don't be surprised when everything takes twice as long as expected to complete—even when someone insists that the task is easy.

To Realize Your Goals, Focus on the Little Picture and the Big Picture

"To know where we are going and what we want; that is order."
—Henri Frédéric Amiel (1821–1881),
Swiss poet and philosopher

Yes, this four-step process requires some self-discipline. You'll see, however, that by putting the details of your plan into order, you can make speedy progress toward your mid-term and long-term goals. Identifying and organizing the details keeps you focused on all the tasks that need to be done, and that's what goal-setting is all about. Use this four-step strategy, and before you know it, you'll be you'll be saying, "I'm finished!"

Little Exercises That Get Big Results

Number Six:
Little Steps That Lead
to Big Goals

Problem-Solving Strategy:
Developing a Flowchart of Steps

*This strategy helps you organize the little steps
that lead to a midterm goal.*

What's the problem? How do you accomplish all the necessary little steps in a midterm goal without having any important details "fall through the cracks?" By creating a flowchart with all the little steps, you can see what needs to be done and when.

What to do: Use the following flowchart to create a sequence of steps to achieve a specific midterm goal. First write in the midterm goal you wish to achieve. Then complete Step One, Step Two, and so on. Finally, write the benefits of achieving this midterm goal.

Midterm goal: _____

_____

Step 1:
_____
_____
_____
_____

Step 2:
_____
_____
_____
_____

Step 3:
_____
_____
_____
_____

Step 4:
_____
_____
_____
_____

Step 5:
_____
_____
_____
_____

Step 6:
_____
_____
_____
_____

Benefits: _____

_____

_____

FOLLOW-UP

Now that you have completed a flowchart of little steps to achieve one midterm goal, revisit the midterm goals (billboards) you listed on page 68. On a separate sheet of paper, create a flowchart for each of your midterm goals. If necessary, you can add more steps to the flowcharts. Keep in mind that you don't need to complete the flowchart for one midterm goal before going onto the next. When ideas come to you for a little step to achieve another midterm goal, then go to that specific flowchart and fill in a box. As a result, you'll quickly organize all the little steps that will lead you to your midterm goals and your big dreams.

Little Things Checklist

Focusing on and achieving all the little steps that lead to your midterm goals is a real challenge, but you can do it if you specifically identify what you want to accomplish. Here are some additional tips to help you organize and execute all the details necessary to achieve your dreams.

- ✔ Keep your flowcharts handy so you can add little steps as you think of them.

- ✔ Add even the smallest details to your flowchart because those are the ones that frequently get overlooked.

- ✔ Consider rearranging the order of your flowchart to see if a different sequence in your order of operations might be more efficient than the one you have written.

- ✔ Use a pencil to fill in your flowchart so you can easily change the content and order of the boxes.

- ✔ If an item in your flowchart requires several steps, it may be a separate midterm goal.

- ✔ Check for and eliminate any duplicated or unnecessary steps on your flowchart.

- ✔ Discipline yourself to complete the flowchart for your midterm goals before you execute them. You won't be sorry.

WHAT YOU'VE LEARNED IN STEP TWO

You know your destination and you have planned the midterm goals that will help you get there. You understand that billboards not only keep you on course, but they allow you to assess your progress and make adjustments in your plan. You have also learned to evaluate and prioritize your midterm goals and be aware of any missing goals that are critical to your success. Now you know how to organize all the little steps necessary to complete your midterm goals into a flow-chart. This visual representation of the overall process allows you to experiment with your ideas by putting your plan into action. Finally, you have learned that by organizing your big and little steps, you will turn haphazard efforts into an organized approach to achieve your dreams.

WHAT'S NEXT?

Now that you have planned your actions, you are ready to go on to Step Three and chapter seven. Your next step is to put your toe in the water and set your plans in motion.

Step Three

ACT ON YOUR PLANS

"It is from numberless diverse acts of courage and belief that human history is shaped. Each time a man stands up for an ideal, or acts to improve the lot of others, or strikes out injustice, he sends forth a tiny ripple of hope."

—Senator Robert F. Kennedy (1925–1968),
American political leader

7

Setting Your Plan in Motion

"You may be disappointed if you fail, but you are doomed if you don't try."

—Beverley Sills (b. 1929),
American operatic soprano
and director of the New York City Opera

ACTOR GEORGE KENNEDY served fourteen years in the army before he decided to retire early and pursue his lifelong dream: a career in acting. Friends and family told Kennedy that he was crazy to leave the security of the military. They reminded him that he had only six more years until he would receive his full retirement benefits package. Some people pointed out that the life of a struggling actor was no picnic and even suggested that it was sheer fantasy to think he could become a movie star at his age. Ignoring the odds and the advice, Kennedy took the plunge and headed for Hollywood. It took hard work and perseverance, but George Kennedy fulfilled his dream. He went on to star in a hit television series and won an Academy Award for his role in the movie *Cool Hand Luke.*

Now is the time for you to take action—any action—that may further your progress. Don't worry about whether you are approaching the task in a perfectly organized way or even whether you're following your midterm goals or billboards. The most important thing is that you do not let inactivity gain a foothold, because the longer you remain "on hold," the harder it is to create momentum.

Don't Let Fear or Past Mistakes Keep You from Taking Action

"If you have made mistakes, there is always another chance for you. And suppose you have tried and failed again and again. You may have a fresh start any moment you choose, for this thing that we call 'failure' is not falling down, but staying down."
—Mary Pickford (1893–1979),
American stage and film actress

Do you have a big dream, and even a plan to achieve it, but still hesitate to take the first steps to turn it into a reality? Are you afraid that you might fail or that others will laugh at you if you fall flat on your face? Have you tried to initiate the first few steps in your plan, only to give up because you didn't get the results you wanted?

If you are still reluctant to pursue your dreams at high speed, then use the following low-risk action strategies to overcome inertia and the fear of rejection. These easy-to-execute steps will help you build the momentum and confidence you need to make identifiable progress toward your long-term goal.

Four Action Strategies
for Reluctant Starters

Action Strategy 1: Make a list of rewarding activities

Action Strategy 2: Choose one rewarding activity
and complete it

Action Strategy 3: Connect the rewarding activity
to a midterm goal

Action Strategy 4: Create an "Activity Sandwich"
of fun and tedious tasks

ACTION STRATEGY ONE:
MAKE A LIST OF REWARDING ACTIVITIES

"Find out what you like doing best and get someone to pay you for doing it."

—Katherine Whitehorn (b. 1929),
British writer and broadcaster

Take a close look at your midterm goals and flowchart from chapters five and six. Identify a few steps that you think are more fun, more interesting, or easier to complete than the rest. Don't worry if the steps you choose are out of sequence or not the most important. The criterion is that the steps must be personally rewarding in some identifiable way. For instance, if your goal is to create a rose garden in your backyard, the activities that are more fun than digging out rocks and roots might be:

- Walking to the library to do research

- Interviewing professional gardeners

- Going online and joining a discussion group with other backyard gardeners

- Reading and organizing all your articles about roses and specialized gardens

- Attending workshops on home garden design and plant care

- Going on a guided tour at a botanical garden

- Taking a walk in a local rose garden

Having a list of enjoyable activities related to your goal can help you in several ways. Let's say you planned to visit a botanical garden and it rains that day. When you have a list of various activities related to your goal, you can quickly choose another, if one is inconvenient. By doing so, you are still pressing forward toward your goal. With your list of your enjoyable tasks ready at your side, you will never have to ask yourself, "What do I do next?"

ACTION STRATEGY TWO: CHOOSE *ONE* REWARDING ACTIVITY AND COMPLETE IT

"I will go anywhere as long as it's forward."
—David Livingstone (1813–1873),
Scottish missionary and explorer

Now is the time to apply the famous athletic shoe company slogan, "Just Do It." Don't let any second-guessing creep into your process and throw you off the track. Remember that what you choose is up to you. But, if you decide to take a walk through a local rose garden for inspiration, be sure to start *and finish* the task.

Choosing only one manageable activity to pursue at a time is important for several reasons. If you frequently get overwhelmed by the many steps necessary to complete a midterm goal, then choosing one rewarding task simplifies the problem. Completing one easy task at a time also builds self-confidence because it shows you can accomplish what you set out to do. Finally, finishing one rewarding activity will motivate you to start and complete other enjoyable tasks. As you accomplish each new task, your momentum will build and so will your ability to succeed.

ACTION STRATEGY THREE:
CONNECT THE REWARDING ACTIVITY
TO A MIDTERM GOAL

"The greatest thing in this world is not so much where we are, but what direction we are moving."
—Oliver Wendell Holmes (1809–1894),
American doctor and author

Making a connection between a rewarding activity and a specific midterm goal reinforces your ability to achieve what you set out to do. To assess the value of the activity, ask yourself questions like the ones following. The answers following each question are examples of what the person dreaming of a back-yard rose garden might offer.

Did I accomplish what I set out to do?

Yes. I wanted to see an example of a well-designed rose garden and I did.

How easy was it to complete the activity?

It took some effort, but completing it was easier than I originally thought. I had to drive forty-five minutes to City Rose Garden. Once I got there, I spent two hours sketching the garden design.

How does the activity fit into my big-picture plans?

The City Rose Garden stimulated my imagination and helped me visualize how my rose garden might look.

In what ways did it help me move closer to a midterm goal?

One of my midterm goals is to design and build a trellis for the climbing roses in my garden. This rose garden had a variety of trellis styles I could adapt and use in my backyard.

Did the activity clarify some issues or bring to light some future obstacles?

My visit to the City Rose Garden made me reconsider the size of my rose garden. I can see now that I will need to allot more space for the climbing roses than I originally thought.

What new insights or opportunities did I gain from the activity?

I was lucky enough to talk to one gardener who told me about a wholesale outlet for garden supplies. In addition, he gave me a cutting from a rare variety of climbing rose. I can't wait to see this little beauty blooming in my rose garden next spring!

Overall, did this activity move me closer to my big goal?

This activity helped me in three ways. First, I now know what kind of trellis I want to build in my backyard rose garden. Second, I have the address of a nursery where I can get the materials I need at a discount. Finally, I have my first prize-winning rose.

Follow up this activity with another from your list of enjoyable tasks or from your flowchart of little steps. Then you can combine a rewarding activity into a series of steps that can boost your rate of progress toward your midterm and long-term goals.

ACTION STRATEGY FOUR: CREATE AN "ACTIVITY SANDWICH" OF FUN AND TEDIOUS TASKS

"Work is much more fun than fun."
—Noël Coward (1899–1973),
English actor, playwright, and composer

It would be great if achieving a goal were as simple as completing enjoyable activities. However, the reality is that to achieve your dreams, you will probably need to complete plenty of less than pleasant tasks, too. One way to maintain your momentum and progress is to "sandwich" one tedious task between two fun tasks. The following example shows how you could categorize several tasks that are necessary to complete a backyard rose garden.

Fun tasks	Tedious tasks
☆ Shop at the nursery	● Rake rocks out of soil
☆ Order the roses	● Spread the manure
☆ Design layout of beds	● Haul 2 × 4s to flower bed
☆ Plant the roses	● Remove the weeds
☆ Build trellis for the roses	● Dig compost into soil

Here is how you can create an "activity sandwich" using three tasks from this list. First complete one fun task and then follow it with one tedious task. Finish making your activity sandwich by choosing another fun task to work on. By sandwiching "one slice of tedium" between "two slices of fun," you will get more accomplished than you ever thought possible. For example:

❑ Shop at the nursery (fun)

❑ Remove the weeds (tedious)

❑ Plant the roses (fun)

Low-Risk Action Strategies Create Momentum and Get Things Done

"Excellence is to do a common thing in an uncommon way."
—Booker T. Washington (1856–1915),
American educator

The secret to making progress on your goals is to squeeze as much motivation as possible from every activity. When you feel good about what you are doing, then you will double your efforts. Between the fun activities, bear down and deal with tedious tasks to get them out of the way. Then you will build up a head of steam that can carry you from one activity to the next and bring you that much closer to achieving your big dream.

LITTLE IDEAS THAT GET BIG RESULTS

Number Seven:
Making an Activity Sandwich

Problem-Solving Strategy:
Sandwiching Tasks

*This strategy helps you overcome inertia by combining
high-interest and low-interest activities.*

What's the problem? When it comes to accomplishing goals, most people prefer to do the enjoyable activities and neglect anything boring or unpleasant. By sandwiching tedious tasks between fun activities, you will complete *all* the steps that lead to your midterm and long-term goals.

What to do: First choose one midterm goal. Then, in the appropriate column, list fun and tedious tasks that you must accomplish to achieve this goal. Finally, make an "activity sandwich" using two tasks from the Fun column and one task from the Tedious column.

Midterm goal: _____

Fun tasks   **Tedious tasks**

☆ _____   💣 _____

☆ _____   💣 _____

☆ _____   💣 _____

☆ _____   💣 _____

☆ _____   💣 _____

☆ _____   💣 _____

ACTIVITY SANDWICH

❑ _____
                          (Fun task)

❑ _____
                          (Tedious task)

❑ _____
                          (Fun task)

FOLLOW-UP

Now you know how to combine fun and tedious tasks so you can get things done and accomplish your goals. Follow up this exercise by looking at your other midterm goals and using the four strategies described in this chapter to initiate some little steps toward each of them. Use a separate sheet of paper to create a list of all the tasks you need to complete in order to achieve each midterm goal. Then make an activity sandwich and start having some fun getting what you want!

Little Things Checklist

Taking the first few steps toward a goal can be intimidating—especially if the steps are tedious or difficult. That's why it's important to focus on the enjoyable activities that will help you achieve your goals. Here are some additional little things you can do to make all your tasks more fun and rewarding.

✔ Always look to see how an enjoyable activity fits into the "big picture" of your long-term goal.

✔ Identify your personal motivators and intersperse them with less enjoyable tasks.

✔ Approach all tasks with the firm intention of completing them.

✔ If possible, delegate necessary tasks that you find tedious or do poorly.

✔ Try to find something enjoyable in every task, even if it is just a sense of satisfaction gained from completing it.

✔ Always keep picking off the little tasks, one at a time, to build momentum and make progress.

✔ Even if you make mistakes, or things do not work out the way you might want, make adjustments and keep at it.

✔ Remember that the only true failure is when you quit attempting to succeed.

WHAT'S NEXT?

Now that you have taken the initiative and started working on the little things that lead to your midterm and long-term goals, you are ready to go on to chapter eight. You will need resources to complete these tasks, so the question is: Where are they going to come from? Your next step is to get your creative juices flowing.

8

Tapping into Your Creativity to Achieve Faster Results

"Get a good idea and stay with it. Dog it, and work at it until it's done, and done right."

—Walt Disney (1901–1966),
American animator and film producer

NEARLY EVERYONE LIVING in America has munched on Cracker Jacks, the candy-coated popcorn and peanut snack, but did you ever wonder how it got to be so popular? It wasn't the only product of this kind on the market—in fact, far from it. By the early 1900s, there were more than one hundred brands of similar-tasting candy, including Yellow Kid, Honey Corn, Little Buster, and Razzle Dazzle, to name just a few. Yet, after nearly a hundred years, only Cracker Jacks still satisfies millions of sweet tooths around the country, while the other brands have long disappeared. Why?

Did Cracker Jacks outlast the other brands of candy-coated popcorn and peanuts because it tasted better? No. Cracker Jacks won the hearts of snack-food lovers because its inventor came up with an innovative marketing idea: He included a small prize in each box. The success story of Cracker Jacks, like so many other success stories, hinged on a stroke of creativity that set this product apart from its competition.

You Can Become an "Idea Person"

Do you wish that you could be more innovative, but you always seem to get stuck doing things the old way? During a department meeting, when your boss asks for suggestions on how to deal with problems, do you wish you could come up with some solutions? Would you like to find more creative approaches to getting over obstacles and achieving your goals? You probably know someone who comes up with one great idea after another, but did you ever wonder how she does it? Many creative problem solvers use a combination of techniques to create, organize, and implement new ideas. They use *brainstorming* to stimulate their imagination and generate ideas. They use an organizational process called *mapping* to provide a framework to connect ideas. Finally, creative people look for new ways to use existing resources. Now you can learn how to expand your creative skills and become an "idea person," too. When you use your imagination, you'll reach your goal sooner and have more fun in the process.

Brainstorming: Generating Ideas and Solutions

"You cannot depend on your eyes when your imagination is out of focus."

—Mark Twain, pseudonym of Samuel Langhorne Clemens (1835–1910), American author and humorist

Webster's Dictionary defines brainstorming as a problem-solving technique that sparks a spontaneous generation of ideas. The purpose of brainstorming is to produce as many solutions, ideas, or outcomes as possible without stopping to evaluate their feasibility or value. Critiquing the ideas occurs later. Brainstorming works through the power of association by offering ideas around a particular subject or problem. The hope is that one idea will lead to another, and another, and so on. Whether you are brainstorming by yourself or with others, follow these five techniques to generate new ideas.

Five Brainstorming Techniques

Technique 1: Focus on one clearly defined idea,
problem, or goal

Technique 2: Build on previous ideas

Technique 3: Generate a large number of ideas

Technique 4: Let one idea lead to another

Technique 5: Record your ideas

TECHNIQUE ONE:
FOCUS ON ONE CLEARLY DEFINED IDEA,
PROBLEM, OR GOAL

If you have not done it already, start by defining the one problem on which you will focus. Brainstorming is most effective when you come up with many possible solutions to overcome one specific obstacle instead of thinking up many unrelated ideas. For example, if you want to change careers, then the focus of your brainstorming could be "find a new job."

TECHNIQUE TWO:
BUILD ON PREVIOUS IDEAS

"An idea is a feat of association."
—Robert Frost (1874–1963), American poet

Another brainstorming technique is to identify ideas or strategies that have worked for you in the past and then come up with ways to make improvements. You don't need to reinvent the wheel to make brainstorming pay off; just do what you do now, only better and more efficiently. For example, let's say a friend of a friend told you about the job, which you now hold. To build on this idea, you can network at a local chamber of commerce or association meeting to expand your contacts and employment possibilities.

TECHNIQUE THREE:
GENERATE A LARGE NUMBER OF IDEAS

"I had never been as resigned to ready-made ideas as I was to ready-made clothes, perhaps because, although I couldn't sew, I could think."
—Jane Rule (b. 1931), American novelist

Successful brainstorming usually generates a large number of ideas, suggestions, and possibilities. The more ideas the brainstorming session produces, the better. You'll have an opportunity to sort out the ideas later. What you don't want to do is to exclude an idea from the brainstorming session, no matter how frivolous it may seem at the time. The reason for this rule is that people often come up with excellent ideas originally intended as a joke. Don't throw these potential gems away.

For example, in the early 1930s, Charles B. Darrow was an unemployed engineer living in Germantown, Pennsylvania. To pass the time and take his mind off his financial problems, Darrow devised an intricate real estate board game played with dice, "deeds," "hotels," and "houses." Daily newspaper accounts of wheeler-dealers winning and losing fortunes in real estate investments spawned the original idea and fed his imagination for the game's components. Then Darrow's visit to the seaside resort of Atlantic City, New Jersey, generated dozens more of ideas for the game, including the names of expensive properties such as "Boardwalk," "Park Place," and "Marvin Gardens."

One day, as Darrow and a few other jobless friends passed another afternoon playing his new game, one fellow joked that he ought to sell it to the game company, Parker Brothers. The rest, as they say, is history. By 1935, Charles Darrow's new board game, "Monopoly," was selling twenty thousand sets a week, and he was on his way to being a millionaire. Today, "Monopoly" is one of the two best-selling board games in the world. (The other is "Scrabble.")

TECHNIQUE FOUR:
LET ONE IDEA LEAD TO ANOTHER

"There is a time when what you're creating and the environment you're creating it in come together."
—Grace Hartigan (b. 1922), American painter

Brainstorming is effective because we make mental associations, or connections, with the words or ideas we think and hear. Words or ideas make us think of more words and ideas. These new thoughts, in turn, lead to another series of words and ideas. If you focus the brainstorming, you can connect these new words and ideas into a defined concept, or even solutions to a problem. Brainstorming is particularly effective when others provide different views, ideas, and solutions around one problem.

For example, I know an amateur photographer who wants to leave his old profession as a social worker and turn his hobby into a vocation. To use this brainstorming technique, he would start with the central problem of how to make money using his photography skills. Then he would think of as many words or ideas as he could that might offer a solution. By letting one idea lead to another and not ruling anything out, the unorganized list might look something like this:

BRAINSTORMING PROBLEM:
HOW CAN I MAKE MONEY SELLING
PHOTOGRAPHS AND
USING MY KNOWLEDGE OF
CAMERAS AND DARKROOM TECHNIQUES?

◆ school and private portraits ◆ promotions ◆ press releases ◆ advertising ◆ newspapers ◆ magazines ◆ posters ◆ travel books ◆ calenders ◆ processing labs ◆ slide shows ◆ gallery shows ◆ postcards ◆ weddings ◆ camera stores ◆ sporting events ◆ animal books and magazines ◆ models ◆ photo archives ◆ teaching at local college or recreation departments ◆ textbooks

Again, the focus on this brainstorming technique is to generate the greatest number of ideas possible *without judging* their viability or practicality. The evaluation and ordering of the ideas happens later.

TECHNIQUE FIVE:
RECORD YOUR IDEAS

"During the night when I cannot sleep, it is on such occasions that my ideas flow best and most abundantly."
—Wolfgang Amadeus Mozart (1756–1791),
Austrian composer

Remember the last time you had a great idea in the middle of the night or while you were jogging, but you neglected to write it down? That great idea is probably lost forever, or at least until you happen to think of it again. Don't let those great ideas—or even little ideas—get away from you. Be sure to write down or tape record your ideas as they pop into your head. Brainstorming can generate many useful ideas, but if you don't capture them, they will drift away like smoke in the wind.

BRAINSTORMING NO-NOS

Remember that the purpose of brainstorming is to generate ideas, so avoid these other idea-squashers:

Don't:

- Evaluate or pass judgment on the ideas as you think of them.

- Immediately reject any ideas even if they have obvious flaws.

- Ignore any ideas, no matter how impractical or impossible they may seem at the time you think of them.

If you are brainstorming with other people, nothing can ruin a creative session faster than an overly competitive atmosphere, crass comment, or tactless remark. Also, avoid these idea-killing phrases during a group brainstorming session:

- "That'll never work."

- "We tried that idea before. It didn't work then, and it won't work now."

- "What in the world are you thinking?"

- "This idea is crazy."

- "It's already been done."

- "I don't think so."

- "It'll be more trouble than it's worth."

- "That's the dumbest thing I've ever heard of."

- "Don't be ridiculous."

- "What planet are you on?"

Measuring the Value of an Idea

"I tune extraneous things out and focus on the task at hand."
—Sandra Day O'Connor (b. 1930),
first woman to serve as a justice of the U.S. Supreme Court

When it comes to brainstorming, there is good news and bad news. The good news is that brainstorming generates lots of ideas and possible solutions to problems. The bad news is that not all the ideas are useful or applicable to your specific goal. Like a gardener who culls weak seedlings from a flower bed, you too must sift through your ideas and focus on the ones with the most potential.

Not all ideas are created equal; some are going to help you achieve your goals more than others. The question is, how do you know which ideas to use now, which ones to save for later, and which ones to discard? Before you rush to judgment, give yourself time to consider how the idea or option will affect your overall plan and goal. Allowing some time to pass gives you a broader perspective on your idea. I use the following two criteria to measure the value of the ideas and solutions after a successful brainstorming session.

CRITERION ONE:
WILL THIS IDEA HELP ME ACHIEVE MY
MIDTERM AND LONG-TERM GOALS?

Not all the ideas you generate—even if they are good ones—will help you achieve your specifically defined goal. To determine if an idea is worthwhile pursuing, ask yourself:

Does this idea fit into my "big-picture" plans, or is it a diversion?

Does this idea sharpen (or does it diffuse) my focus on my midterm and long-term goals?

Do I have the skills and resources to make this idea workable?

How easy is it to put this idea into practice?

Will this idea save me time and/or money?

Is this idea safe?

Will this idea help eliminate wasted effort and
resources?

Is this idea consistent with my values?

CRITERION TWO:
IS NOW THE RIGHT TIME
TO PUT THIS IDEA INTO ACTION?

Poor timing probably accounts for the failure of more ideas
than just about anything else. You might have a good idea, but
the timing may be wrong. To help you decide if your idea is
timely or not, ask yourself:

How will I benefit from this idea if I act now?

How will acting on this idea affect the rest of my plan?

What opportunities may present themselves if I act on
this idea now?

What are the pros and cons of acting on this idea now?

Will this idea be easier or more difficult to act upon if
I wait?

How might external forces such as the weather, business
climate, or availability of materials affect the success of
this idea?

Is my timing critical to the success of this idea?

Separate the Wheat from the Chaff

*"To make ideas effective, we must be able to fire them off. We must
put them into action."*
—Virginia Woolf (1882–1941), English author

It's not always easy to differentiate the good idea from the clunker. Someone may hesitate to discard any idea, no matter how impractical it may be, simply because she thought of it. Or, a pessimist's rigid views or fears can throw cold water on a potentially valuable idea. Usually, you will need to test your idea to learn if it will pay off for you. Once you decide that an idea has potential value, your next step in expanding your creative skills is to organize all its related components.

Mapping Organizes Your Ideas Visually

"Take an object. Do something to it. Do anything else to it."
—Jasper Johns (b. 1930), American artist

The technique of "mapping" is a fast and creative way to organize random ideas on paper using words, boxes, lines, symbols, colors, and even pictures. This is a departure from the traditional method of organizing information in Roman numeral outline form. When you use a formal outline, you establish the framework first, and then fill in the ideas beside the letters and numbers. Mapping works the other way around. It takes advantage of a tendency that many creative people have to think of ideas "out of order." By mapping, you can organize these random thoughts and ideas without curtailing the creative process. When I write a book, I use the following combination of brainstorming and mapping to generate and organize my ideas.

The following examples use mapping to organize ideas on how to go about finding a new job. See how the map grows in each step.

ABCs of Mapping

A = Address your central idea, problem, or goal

B = Brainstorm a random list of ideas, solutions,
steps, etc.

C = Collect the main ideas into boxes around central
idea, problem, or goal

A = ADDRESS YOUR CENTRAL IDEA, PROBLEM, OR GOAL

Write a key word that represents a main idea, problem, or goal in a box in the middle of a sheet of paper. For example, if you are looking for employment in the computer field, you could write:

Finding a job in computers

B = BRAINSTORM A RANDOM LIST OF IDEAS, SOLUTIONS, STEPS, ETC.

Now you can apply the brainstorming techniques you learned in the first part of this chapter. Write down as many ideas as possible, but don't evaluate them until later. A job seeker's list of random ideas might look like this:

- Get additional computer training

- Interview with job recruiters

- Network for job leads

- Go on an information interview

- Call human resources at target companies

- Check local colleges for computer classes

- Attend industry association meetings

- Improve interviewing skills

- Talk to friends in the business

- Get coaching for public speaking

- Check media for stories on growth industries

- Buy a used computer to practice on and get freelance work

- Attend a workshop to improve networking skills

- Ask a friend for tips on using a new computer software program

- Practice mock interviews using a video camera

- Research job market

C = COLLECT THE MAIN IDEAS INTO BOXES AROUND THE CENTRAL IDEA, PROBLEM, OR GOAL

Now take the random list of ideas and make an organized map around a central box. I always look at my list for the main ideas and place those in satellite boxes around my central idea or goal. For the job seeker, these main ideas might be: getting computer training; researching the job market; improving interviewing skills; and networking for job leads. The central idea with its satellite boxes and ideas would look like this:

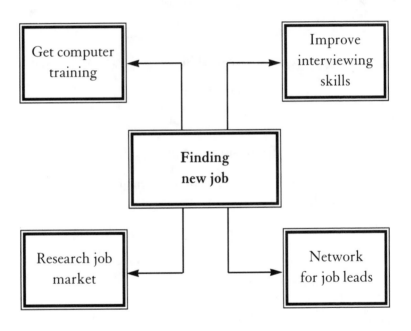

Then write each additional idea around the main idea that relates to it. The following map shows how a map can organize the job seeker's random list of sixteen ideas, solutions, steps, and so on. You'll get a chance to map your own ideas in the exercise at the end of this chapter.

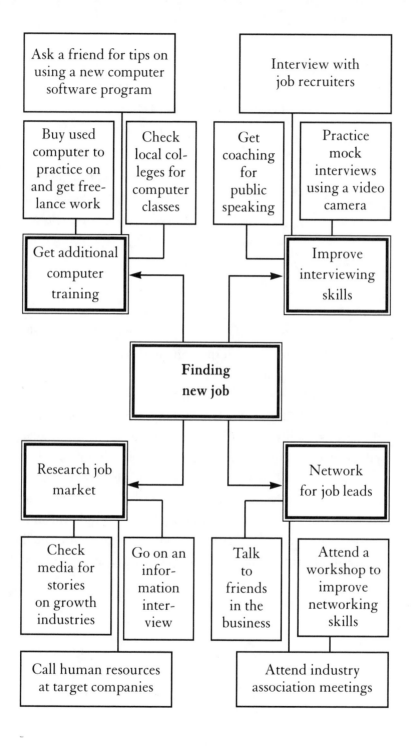

Brainstorming and Mapping Bring All Your Ideas into Perspective

"I walked up the Kahlenberg, and when it got hot and I got hungry, I sat down by a little brook and unpacked my Swiss sandwich. And just as I opened the greasy paper, that darn tune pops into my head."
—Anton Bruckner (1824–1896),
Austrian composer, when asked how he thought of the motif
for his Ninth Symphony

Mapping helps you see the big picture along with the little picture. It helps organize all those great ideas you have brainstormed into a format that you can see. By creating a map of your goals and ideas, you can see what pieces of your plan are in place and which ones are still missing. Although stretching your creative skills can be great fun, be sure that the results facilitate progress toward your goal. Keep your brainstorming and mapping focused around one central idea, problem, or goal. Once you develop your map, then follow up with the necessary steps that move you closer to your midterm and long-term goals. As you exercise your creative skills, you'll discover that great untapped resource for ideas and solutions: your imagination.

LITTLE EXERCISES THAT GET BIG RESULTS

Number Eight:
Mapping Your Ideas

Problem-Solving Strategy:
Making an Ideas Map

This strategy helps you organize many of your ideas
into a visual format so you can see
how they relate to one another.

What's the problem? Getting all your ideas organized can seem like an impossible task. When you make an ideas map, you can see the relationships and overall structure of the key components that make up your goals.

What to do: Write a long-term goal and four midterm goals in the boxes in the center of the map. On a separate sheet of paper, brainstorm and list as many ideas as you can that relate to your goals. Don't evaluate, limit, or order your ideas. Next, take the ideas from your list and organize them on your ideas map.

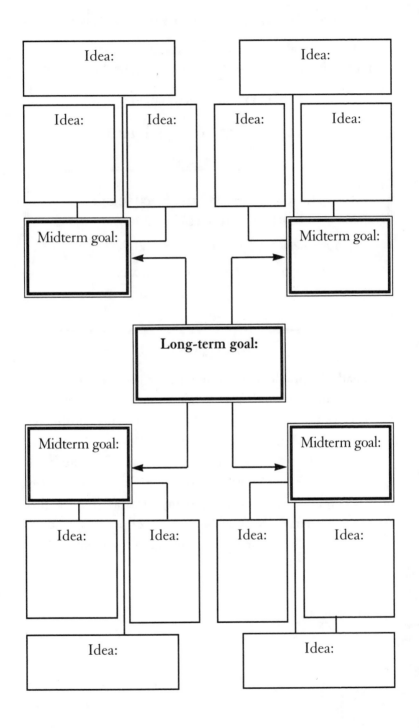

FOLLOW-UP

Now you know how to use an ideas map to organize all your key ideas around your midterm and long-term goals. Your next step is to create another ideas map for each of your midterm goals. On a new sheet of paper, draw a new map, place one midterm goal in the center box, and start the brainstorming process again. Soon you'll be thinking of so many ideas and they will be so well organized that you'll be putting them into action faster than you ever imagined possible.

Little Things Checklist

Generating and organizing lots of ideas can stimulate your imagination and lead to measurable results. The following tips will also help increase your creative skills and speed your progress toward your goals.

- ✔ Modify or adapt a tool or resource to solve a new problem.

- ✔ Use every resource you have to its maximum.

- ✔ Simplify a complicated method to save time and money.

- ✔ Rearrange your resources to use them more effectively.

- ✔ Look to see how you can use one resource to solve two problems.

- ✔ Add a new twist to an old idea.

- ✔ Always seek new ways to use old resources.

- ✔ Reverse the order of how you do things and see if you get better results.

- ✔ Substitute new ideas for old ways of doing things that have lost their effectiveness.

- ✔ Look for ways to combine two old ideas to solve one new problem.

- ✔ Keep looking for little ideas; they lead to big break-throughs.

WHAT'S NEXT?

Since you know how to tap into your creative skills to speed up your progress, you're ready to go on to chapter nine. Your next step is to work hard without burning yourself out.

9

Pacing Strategies to Help You
Go the Distance

"The greatest athletes want it so much, they run themselves to death.
You've got to have an obsession, but if unchecked, it's destructive."
—Alberto Salazar (b. 1958),
American runner, winner of New York City Marathon
in 1980, 1981, and 1982

AMERICAN MARATHON RUNNER Mary Decker Slaney has
always taken her training seriously, but now she paces
herself to avoid what has been a major threat to her career—
chronic fatigue and injury. In the past, when Slaney trained
too hard for too long, she won races—she holds five American
long distance running records—but at a high price. She frequently got sick or hurt during her training or after the race.
Slaney has learned this lesson the hard way, suffering through
nearly twenty operations to correct running-induced injuries.
Determined not to end her long and brilliant career, she began
to follow a rigid program of controlled workouts and gradually increased the distances she ran. As a result, at age thirty-
seven she remained physically healthy and qualified at the
5,000 meters for the 1996 Olympic trials.

When the day for the big race arrived, Mary knew that
pacing herself for the previous months had paid off. She was

in great shape and ready to compete against the world's best women runners. Then came the tensest moment in the race and the one that tested her strength, self-discipline, and perseverance. As Mary and the other lead runners entered the final stretch to the finish line, one fierce competitor bumped into her. Stumbling and nearly falling down, Mary somehow

---

Eight Pacing Strategies

Pacing Strategy 1: Make a long-distance game plan

Pacing Strategy 2: Use "splits" to divide your efforts into equal parts

Pacing Strategy 3: Warm up before starting a difficult task

Pacing Strategy 4: Record your progress to build momentum

Pacing Strategy 5: Use the "hard-easy" system to reduce fatigue

Pacing Strategy 6: Selectively cross-train to build strength

Pacing Strategy 7: Use "peaking" and "tapering" to optimize performance

Pacing Strategy 8: Save a burst of energy for a strong finish

---

regained her balance and ran even harder to capture second place and a silver medal.

Marathon Strategies Can Help You Complete Your Goals

"Keep breathing."
—Sophie Tucker (1884–1966),
American singer's advice on how to last in show business

As the story about Mary Decker Slaney illustrates, winning marathon runners don't just go out and run a long distance race at the drop of a hat; they train for months. They know that strength, discipline, and endurance determine how successfully they will run the race. The same rules apply to you when you undertake a major endeavor. Setting the right pace increases your chances of completing your goal. Use these eight pacing strategies while pursuing your midterm and long-term goals and you'll come out a winner.

PACING STRATEGY ONE: MAKE A LONG-DISTANCE GAME PLAN

"If you fail to plan, you are planning to fail."
—proverb

Most runners consider how they are going to run their race long before the starting gun sounds. Perhaps they will set the pace for the other runners, or follow on the heels of their rival. Maybe they will stay in the middle of the pack until they see an opportunity and then move ahead. Experienced runners normally do not sprint from the beginning of a long race because they know that they must conserve their energy if they want to cross the finish line. They also know that toward the end of the race, they will need to draw on their energy reserves for that all-important push to the finish line.

Perhaps your dream is to earn a college degree, buy a home, or travel to an exotic place. The idea here is to pace yourself with a long-distance game plan. What does a long-distance game plan look like? It doesn't need to be elaborate, just specific. For example, I met a woman who worked as a full-time assistant manager in a large hotel while she was studying to be a court recorder. She described her long-distance game plan this way: "Since my goal will take about two years to achieve, I'll continue to work here and take three classes each semester until I complete my degree. That way, I'll change careers without killing myself in the process."

By adopting a long-distance game plan, you can pace yourself for each midterm goal and increase your chances of completing your long-term goal on schedule. If, however, you simply go all out for the finish line without pacing yourself for the long haul, you are likely to run out of energy long before you reach your final goal.

PACING STRATEGY TWO:
USE "SPLITS" TO DIVIDE YOUR EFFORTS
INTO EQUAL PARTS

The "split" is another pacing strategy used by runners. The idea is to run each half of the race in about the same time. This strategy helps the runners keep their speed in check so they have sufficient energy at the end of the race to surge across the finish line, and hopefully to win. The beauty of this strategy for a goal seeker like you is that you can achieve steady progress toward your goal without becoming overly fatigued near the end.

Like all pacing, the split strategy requires self-discipline. In the first half of your project you may feel tempted to push yourself to the limit, but you'll need to hold yourself back and conserve your energy. For example, I knew a person who started project after project, but rarely finished anything. He began the job like gangbusters, working so hard that you'd think that nothing could stop him. About halfway through his efforts, however, he inevitably got so exhausted that he would quit. If he had learned to use a split pacing strategy, he could have broken this frustrating pattern of burning out. Then he would have had the reserves he needed to maintain his progress from the beginning to the end of his projects.

I use a split strategy when I write books. In the year or so it takes me to write a book, I split my efforts into two six-month blocks of time. My midterm goal for the first split is to research, write, and revise one complete draft of the book. My goal for the second split is to revise the complete manuscript three more times and then do the final polish. A split strategy gives me the flexibility I need when I write a book. For example, if I don't write as many chapters as I originally projected in the first split, then I can write the outstanding chapters in the second split. This strategy also gives me enough energy at the end of the project to handle any snags and add the final touches to make the book as good as possible.

You can also use a split strategy to achieve your midterm goals, too. For example, if you want to complete a midterm goal in one month, then pace yourself by organizing your little steps and tasks into two splits of two weeks each. If you meet your objectives in your first split, then chances are you'll complete the remaining tasks in the second split.

PACING STRATEGY THREE:
WARM UP BEFORE STARTING
A DIFFICULT TASK

Every runner knows that plunging into a hard physical workout without first stretching exercises is asking for trouble. To skip warming up can result in pulled muscles or some other painful injury that can take him or her out of the race. Warming up with the proper exercises helps eliminate this problem. When it comes to tackling any obstacle, taking a few minutes to warm up before you start your efforts usually makes moderate and difficult tasks a little easier. For example, before I start a long day of writing, I usually warm up for about fifteen minutes with the *New York Times* crossword puzzle. It's fun, challenging, and gets my brain working in the morning so I can focus on the tough job ahead. If I don't spend a few minutes with the crossword, it isn't the end of the world. However, instead of fifteen minutes to really focus my thoughts, it might take me a half hour. At that rate, it would take me an extra hour and fifteen minutes a week to get down to work.

While this pacing strategy may not apply to all long-term goals, you can use it for midterm and short-term goals. Let's say, for example, that today is Monday and that you have a big job interview scheduled Friday. You could use these warm-ups to help you prepare for your interview.

Interview Warm-Ups

Monday: Review your résumé and the description of the job for which you are applying.

Tuesday: Use a mirror to practice introducing yourself and to check that your body language is receptive and businesslike.

Wednesday: Practice saying three reasons why you're the best person for the job.

Thursday: Conduct a mock interview with a friend or speech trainer.

Friday: Arrive twenty minutes early to take a short walk before the interview to gather your thoughts, relax, and visit the restroom to check your appearance.

Try warming up before you dive headlong into a difficult task or step. The best warm-ups are fun, easy, fast, and limber you up mentally or physically for the tasks you are about to perform.

PACING STRATEGY FOUR:
RECORD YOUR PROGRESS
TO BUILD MOMENTUM

Momentum is the feeling of power that sustains drive, commitment, and progress. To help build their momentum before a race, runners often record their workout times so they can see steady progress toward their targeted running goals. You can use the same strategy to help you achieve your long-term goals. For example, I know that I can consistently write about four manuscript pages a day. Based on that rate of progress, I can estimate about how long it will take me to write a chapter, and, ultimately, an entire book. I always work with a writing schedule and record my rate of progress. That way I can see if I am pacing myself correctly. In addition, I get the satisfaction of seeing the little check marks on my schedule as I finish writing or editing each chapter.

Keeping simple records also helps establish consistency and builds momentum. Some mornings you might feel like doing anything but working on your project. Keeping records can help motivate you to complete a task, even when you'd rather be doing something—anything—else. For example, I have a friend who insists on jogging every day. To build momentum and self-discipline, he puts a small sticker of a bright yellow running shoe on his calender for each day he runs. His record is fifty-six days in a row. My friend jogs when he doesn't feel like it and even in poor weather because he doesn't want to start over trying to break his record.

PACING STRATEGY FIVE:
USE THE "HARD-EASY" SYSTEM
TO REDUCE FATIGUE

Chronic fatigue and injury are a runner's greatest threats. That is why track coach Bill Bowerman developed the "hard-easy" training system. He knew that rest was as important a part of successful conditioning as exercise. Using this system, a runner trains hard one day, then eases off the next day or two. On the third day, she trains hard again. Bowerman found that runners who used this method progressed faster with fewer injuries, and they avoided chronic fatigue.

Like the long-distance runner, chronic fatigue and illness can threaten your goals, too. Adapting a hard-easy training system can help you avoid these problems and speed your progress toward your midterm and long-term goals. In the exercises at the end of chapters five and six, you listed several steps you need to take to reach your goal. When you take a closer look at these steps, you'll see that some are more difficult than others. If you focus on the one difficult task every few days with moderate and easy tasks slotted between, you'll avoid burning out before reaching your goal. For example, I use a hard-easy work schedule in the beginning of a book writing project. It looks something like this:

Gabor's Weekly "Hard-Easy" Work Schedule

Goal for the week:

Write, edit, and polish one book chapter

	Task	Level of difficulty
Mon.	*Research chapter*	*Easy-moderate*
Tues.	*Outline chapter*	*Moderate-difficult*
Wed.	*Write first draft of chapter*	*Difficult*
Thurs.	*Edit chapter*	*Difficult-moderate*
Fri.	*Write second draft of chapter*	*Moderate-easy*

PACING STRATEGY SIX:
CROSS-TRAIN TO BUILD STRENGTH

In his book *Iron and Silk,* Mark Salzman tells about his experiences teaching English in China and studying in with several martial arts masters. One teacher suggested that Salzman learn calligraphy to supplement his martial arts training. The teacher believed that mastering calligraphy and martial arts required many of the same skills and discipline, and that developing a facility in one would enhance ability in the other. Judging from Salzman's public performance at the 1985 National Martial Arts Competition and Conference in Tianjin, China, his cross-training paid off.

Cross-training is a technique that many runners and other athletes use to build strength, complement their workouts, or help recover from injuries. For example, if running the marathon is a runner's primary goal, cross-training could include bicycling, roller skating, cross-country skiing, and swimming. The philosophy behind cross-training is that it can become tiresome to do one thing—whether it is running, writing, or job hunting—all the time. Cross-training provides variety and an opportunity to enhance your abilities while avoiding chronic fatigue and boredom.

You can use cross-training techniques to help you achieve your goals, too. However, choosing cross-training activities requires common sense and purpose. If you have a particular weakness that hinders your progress, then a specific cross-training exercise or activity may be the answer. For example, while I write mostly nonfiction, I am working on a fiction project that helps me improve my descriptive writing skills. I also cross-train by presenting workshops and keynote speeches to discuss the subjects that I write books about.

If you have started a new business, for instance, then possible cross-training activities might include:

- ◆ Reading a small business handbook
- ◆ Taking a "marketing your business" seminar
- ◆ Giving a speech at a chamber of commerce meeting
- ◆ Volunteering your services to associations related to your business
- ◆ Learning a customer database management program on the computer

BE SELECTIVE WHEN CHOOSING CROSS-TRAINING ACTIVITIES

The secret to choosing the right cross-training activity is to make sure that it complements and supplements other specific activities that lead to your midterm and long-term goals. Avoid cross-training activities that require too much time or effort, because they can distract you from your primary goal. Above all, keep in mind that cross-training is not a substitute for rest, relaxation, and leisure activities.

PACING STRATEGY SEVEN: USE "PEAKING" AND "TAPERING" TO OPTIMIZE PERFORMANCE

"I don't know anyone who has got to the top without hard work. That is the recipe."
—Margaret Thatcher (b. 1925), British political leader
and first woman elected prime minister of England

When I was a first-year college student, my study habits were not very productive. I remember cramming for days before taking a particularly tough economics test. Like many students, I continued to hit the books most of the night before dragging myself into class blurry-eyed the next morning for the exam. Much to my dismay, I did poorly on my exam and was frustrated with my grade. After discussing the test and my study habits with my teacher, he suggested I try a different strategy for the next midterm exam. He told me to gradually increase how much time I studied each day up to four days before the test. Then start decreasing my study time and stop studying entirely for eight hours before taking the test. This strategy, he explained, would allow me to pace myself so I would be fresh for the exam. It made sense, so I tried it. What a difference it made in taking the next test. Not only did this teacher's advice help me through college, but it still serves me today when I set out to achieve long-term goals.

Runners often use this strategy—called "peaking and tapering"—to race at their optimum on a particular day. "Peaking" means to increase the intensity and frequency of the effort you make until you reach your maximum ability to perform. "Tapering" means to decrease the intensity and frequency of your efforts so that your body and mind have enough time to rest before performing at their optimum on another day. A peaking and tapering strategy focuses on the times to push harder and the times to back off.

Peaking and tapering strategies will help you achieve better results over long periods of time with less effort. To use this strategy effectively, be sure to:

◆   Know when you need to perform your best.

◆   Schedule your peak to meet your performance requirements.

◆　Systematically increase the intensity and frequency of your efforts to build your strength.

◆　Know your limits and err on the side of caution so you don't become sick or injure yourself.

◆　Taper off the intensity and frequency of your efforts as you approach your peak.

◆　Rest before making your optimum effort.

PACING STRATEGY EIGHT: SAVE A BURST OF ENERGY FOR A STRONG FINISH

Marathon runners know that the final miles of a race require more physical and psychological effort just to keep an even pace. In a close contest, however, a runner must sprint to the finish line if he expects to win. The same principle is true in nearly any endeavor that places heavy demands on your time and energy.

Even if you have paced yourself, to achieve your best you probably will need to tap into your energy reserves as you approach the end of your project. In the final stretch, you will need to work longer hours, concentrate harder, and be more patient and disciplined. When you are so close to the end of your project that you see the finish line, it can be tempting to overlook some remaining details. Nothing could be more detrimental to your success than to diffuse your focus at this critical time.

For example, in the final few weeks of a book writing project, I'm tired and want to be done with the job. However, no matter how much I feel like stopping, I work even harder until I reach the due date—my finish line. Like the marathon runner near the end of the race, I dig deep into my reserves and do everything possible to finish with a burst of energy. I keep saying to myself, "Stay focused and kick hard until the end." Afterward, I can relax and say to myself, "I gave the job my best shot."

Mix and Match Pacing Strategies

"Even pace running is the best way to get the best out of yourself."
—Arthur Lydiard (b. 1917),
New Zealand running coach and author

As you set out to achieve your goals, mix and match these eight pacing strategies to fit your particular needs. You can also adapt these strategies to help yourself over a troublesome hurdle that has impeded your progress in the past. Test the strategies and get a sense of which ones blend most naturally with your work style. Choose the ones that work the best for you. In the end, no matter which pacing strategies you use, they will help you make steady progress in completing the little tasks and achieving your big goals.

Number Nine:
Pacing Yourself
for the Long Haul

Problem-Solving Strategy:
Making a "Hard-Easy"
Pacing Chart

This strategy helps you organize and schedule easy,
moderate, and difficult tasks so that you can achieve
your goals without suffering chronic fatigue.

What's the problem? Even highly motivated achievers can get disheartened, overtired, or sick if they fail to pace themselves. Creating and following a "hard-easy" training schedule builds your strength and endurance while you strive to complete your midterm goals on a daily basis.

What to do: First use the "hard-easy" pacing chart to categorize all the tasks that you must complete to achieve a midterm goal. Then complete the pacing schedule based on your own timetable and availability. Circle the level of difficulty for each task you list.

My midterm goal is: _____

_____

Hard tasks   Easy tasks

_____   _____
_____   _____
_____   _____

Hard-Easy Pacing Chart

Moderately hard tasks   Moderately easy tasks

_____   _____
_____   _____
_____   _____

Hard-Easy Schedule for Week of _____

Midterm goal for the week: _____

Days	Task	Level of difficulty
Mon:		*Easy/moderate/difficult*
Tues:		*Easy/moderate/difficult*
Wed:		*Easy/moderate/difficult*
Thurs:		*Easy/moderate/difficult*
Fri:		*Easy/moderate/difficult*

Note: Finding the time necessary to complete the tasks on your hard-easy schedule may be a challenge. Make an effort to *complete at least one easy task* even on the days when you have little time to devote to the job. The most important part of this pacing strategy is that you work steadily to achieve your midterm and long-term goals.

FOLLOW-UP

Now that you know how to organize tasks with varying levels of difficulty into a "hard-easy" pacing schedule, try juggling their order. For example, perhaps after experimenting, you find that you prefer to focus on your most difficult task the first thing Monday or Tuesday. Then you can leave the easier tasks for the rest of the week. Find out what combination of the "hard-easy" strategy works best for you. However, if you leave difficult tasks for late in the day or the week, you might run out of steam or end up using your most creative and productive times on less demanding activities.

Little Things Checklist

Making steady progress on your midterm and long-term goals takes patience and self-discipline. The following tips can help you stay on track without burning out.

✔ The longer the project and more difficult the goal, the more important it is to follow a disciplined pacing strategy.

✔ Experiment with different combinations of pacing strategies to see which ones work best for you.

✔ Observe and talk to productive people to find out how they get things done without getting overtired or becoming sick.

✔ Keep tuned into your body so you know when you are approaching your physical, emotional, and mental limits. If you become fatigued, then stop. Rest a short time and then restart your efforts.

✔ The ideal starting pace is the one you can maintain throughout the project. At first the pace you set will seem easy, but it will become progressively more difficult, especially toward the end of your project.

WHAT YOU'VE LEARNED IN STEP THREE

In the last three chapters you learned how to act on your plan. You know four action strategies to help you get over the initial hurdle of starting your project. You've learned how to get all the tasks done by sandwiching enjoyable tasks with those that are tedious. You've discovered how to brainstorm plenty of ideas without prejudging their value or feasibility. You've seen how to create a map of your ideas so you can get the job done. Finally, you've learned eight pacing strategies—based on those used by marathon runners—to help you cross the finish line and complete your projects.

WHAT'S NEXT?

Now that you have set your plan in motion, you're ready to go on to Step Four and chapter ten. Your next step is using criticism to help you achieve your goals.

Step Four

PERSEVERE, PERSEVERE, PERSEVERE

"Don't give up. Keep going. There is always a chance that you will stumble onto something terrific. I have never heard of anyone stumbling over anything while he was sitting down."

—Charles Kettering (1876–1958),
American inventor and
cofounder of Delco Electronics

10

Using Criticism
to Overcome Obstacles

"A successful man is one who can lay a firm foundation with the bricks that others throw at him."
—David Brinkley (b. 1920),
American broadcast journalist

OST PEOPLE HAVE heard unkind or critical words about their work or goals. The difference between people who achieve their goals and those who do not depends a great deal on how they view and use criticism. Most successful people welcome constructive criticism. By extracting valid points and suggestions from criticism, they learn, improve, and continue to press on toward their goal. At the same time, successful people often ignore pessimists, skeptics, and unsolicited or uninformed criticism. Oversensitive people, on the other hand, let the criticism from others—constructive or not—sap their enthusiasm and deflate their confidence. As a result, these people often stop working and ultimately give up on achieving their dreams.

Don't Give Up Just Because
Someone Criticizes Your Work

"Rest satisfied with doing well, and leave others to talk of you as they please."

—Pythagorus (c.580–c.500 B.C.),

Greek philosopher and mathematician

Dealing with criticism can be painful, but it is a big mistake to quit an endeavor just because someone criticizes you or what you are trying to accomplish. Instead of throwing in the towel, take a deep breath. Then determine whether the criticism is constructive and how to relate to it. Use this two-step plan in deciding whether to accept or reject criticism.

Two Steps to Evaluate Criticism

Step 1: Assess the Critic's Knowledge and Motivation

Step 2: Measure the Value of the Criticism

STEP ONE:
ASSESS THE CRITIC'S KNOWLEDGE
AND MOTIVATION

As hard as criticism may be to accept, it can help you to overcome hurdles and may speed your progress to get what you want. The trick is knowing how to evaluate and apply the advice that people offer you. Therefore, assess the source of the criticism before taking action. When criticism comes from a knowledgeable and well-meaning source, it can help you achieve your goals. However, if criticism is uninformed, it can do more harm than good. People who make snide remarks may have a hidden agenda or may want to test your confidence. Of course, when others tease you in a friendly way, take the jest with the spirit in which they intend it. To decide whether to accept or reject criticism, ask yourself:

Does the critic have knowledge or experience in this area?

If the answer is *yes:* Listen carefully when the criticism comes from knowledgeable sources such as coaches, teachers, professionals in the field, coworkers, or supervisors. You might not follow all their advice, but chances are you can profit from their experience and willingness to help you achieve your goals. For example, when the actress Ingrid Bergman complained to director Alfred Hitchcock that she couldn't play a particular scene in a natural way, he advised her to "fake it." Bergman later said that this was the best acting advice she received in her career.

But if the answer is *no:* Know-it-alls, "wanna-bes," dilettantes, and pessimists offer unsolicited advice in areas in which they have little experience. Politely thank them for their input, but ignore their comments and suggestions. For example, Edgar Allan Poe's grotesque stories and morbid poems elicited showers of criticism from the shocked and offended literary establishment of the time. In spite of their opinions, Poe's macabre poem, "The Raven," won him immediate fame with readers throughout the world and is still considered a "classic" of American literature.

Are the critic's comments sincere?

If the answer is *yes:* Listen carefully to the people with constructive criticism who sincerely want to help you succeed.

They may not be the most knowledgeable, but if their concern and motivation are squarely in your corner, then their ideas may be helpful. Keep in mind that even friendly teasing is a way for others to show they support your efforts. For example, Buddy Hackett and fellow comedian Jimmy Durante had just finished eighteen holes of golf. With a score of more than 200, Durante obviously had little talent for the game. When Durante asked what he should give the caddy for a tip, Hackett replied, "Your clubs."

If the answer is *no:* Some rivals and competitors may criticize your efforts or make sarcastic remarks simply to undermine your confidence and motivation. If you value the relationship, you may want to uncover the real reasons behind the negative comments so you can discuss them. If, however, you have no special connection to this individual, ignore him. For example, during the early years of her long and successful film career, Katharine Hepburn received several unflattering reviews. At one point, critics called her "boring" and "box office poison." Fortunately, she didn't let these unkind words stop her from acting or winning four Academy Awards.

Did you ask for feedback?

If the answer is *yes:* If you asked for an honest assessment of your work, then be prepared to hear a lot of criticism and, if you are lucky, some praise. Remember that you do not need to *agree* with the other person's opinion or follow all of her suggestions. Just listen with an open mind and put into practice the points that seem helpful. For example, when Ed Koch was mayor of New York City, he frequently asked New Yorkers, "How am I doing?" The praise and criticism he heard kept him in office from 1978 to 1990.

But if the answer is *no:* Some people insist on offering their comments because they believe it is their duty to be "100 percent truthful" with their opinions. While occasionally their comments may be insightful, more often their harsh words are demoralizing and damaging. For example, I know a fellow to whom an "honest friend" once said, "You don't have what it takes to be an artist, so don't even bother trying." Unfortunately, this fellow took this unsolicited and tactless comment to heart. He never pursued his dream of a career in the fine arts, although he was loaded with talent and ideas. Never let an unsolicited opinion cause you to give up on your dreams.

Does the critical person really want you to succeed?

If the answer is *yes:* Parents, family members, friends, teachers, and some peers may offer constructive criticism as a way to contribute to your success. Listen carefully to their comments and put into practice any ideas that you think will help you overcome the obstacles that stand between you and your goals. For example, the veteran pianist Artur Schnabel gave the budding teenage concert pianist Vladimir Horowitz this helpful advice: "When a piece gets difficult, make faces." Even at the age of 81, when Vladimir Horowitz was taping *The Studio Recordings—New York 1985,* he still made faces. Although in this recording session, most of the faces were joyful ones.

If the answer is *no:* People who gave up on their own dreams (or never had them in the first place) often criticize the efforts of others. Their negative comments reveal more about their own insecurities than anything you may be doing wrong. Don't let their criticism hurt your feelings or prevent you from pursuing your goals. For example, at first Henry Fonda's father did not support his son's decision to become an actor. However, after attending Henry's debut performance, his father reluctantly admitted, "He was perfect."

STEP TWO:
MEASURE THE VALUE OF THE CRITICISM

Some people know what they are talking about, but others just like to hear the sound of their own voices. How do you know if a person's criticism is worthwhile or off-base? The following questions can help you answer this vital question.

Is the advice applicable for your situation?

What might be good advice for someone else could be wrong for your situation. For instance, in 1963, Mary Kay Ash's husband died only a month after investing their life savings in their new company. Her attorney and advisors suggested that she sell her investment and get out of the cosmetics business. For someone else, this advice may have been correct, but Mary Kay decided not to give up on her dream of running her own business. As a result, she built one of the world's largest cosmetic companies.

When it comes to following advice, always trust your instincts. Only *you* know what is right for your situation. If the person's suggestions or criticisms seem helpful, then consider following the recommendations that move you closer to your goals.

Have external circumstances changed?

Always consider external circumstances such as market supply, demand, and timing when assessing the value of criticism. In other words, what may have been good advice last year could be bad now. Consider the father who criticized his son's decision to attend a culinary institute rather than go to law school. "For crying out loud, you can do a lot better than flipping hamburgers for a living! Think of the money you'll make at a big law firm," he said. "They'll hire you the minute you step out of law school."

The father, however, was unaware of changing circumstances in the law profession when he offered his son this advice. During the 1970s and 1980s, attending law school was a popular and lucrative career choice for many college graduates. By the 1990s, however, many law firms suspended new hires, and the market became flooded with experienced attorneys looking for work. Demand for new lawyers had declined to the point that many law school graduates—even those from top Ivy League schools—spent close to a year looking for their first position in a firm. On the other hand, job recruiters expected the demand for highly skilled people in the restaurant, hotel, and hospitality industries to grow well into the next century.

If the person's criticism or advice allows for fluctuations in external circumstances, listen carefully and consider following some of his suggestions. Then use the criticism in deciding how best to achieve your goals.

What supporting evidence does the critic offer?

Before I moved to New York City, someone chided me for even considering moving to "such a terrible place." She told me New York was "dirty, full of crime, and filled with rude people." I was curious how she formed such a negative opinion of the Big Apple, knowing that she had never visited the city. I asked, "How do you know, if you have never been there?" She answered, "Well, I know people who have and that is what they say!" Her lack of personal experience diminished the credibility of her views. As a result, I put little credence in her opinion and did not let it influence my decision to move to New York.

Can the critic back up her criticism with personal experience and facts, or is it merely hearsay or personal opinion? To find out, you can ask:

"Why do you think so?"

"Have you had some experience with this?"

"On what do you base your opinion?"

If the critic can support her criticism or opinion, then listen carefully and consider what she has to say. Then put the criticism to work to help you achieve your goals.

Does the critic share a similar set of values?

In this situation, like many others, the difference in opinions may be due to a different set or values or criteria. For example, when it comes to dining, some people prefer restaurants that serve generous portions. If their plates are overflowing with food, they are happy. Other diners prefer small portions and like to nibble on a variety of tasty dishes. The difference is, one group values the quantity of the food, while the other values its quality. Both groups may describe the places they dine as excellent, while criticizing each other's choice of restaurant.

This issue hit home for a friend who told me about an encounter with someone in the music business. My friend is a talented singer and guitarist who wanted to record an album of American folk songs for children. After hearing a few of my friend's songs, a music executive ridiculed my friend's musical tastes and called him old-fashioned. "Actually," the executive said afterward, "I never really liked folk music, anyway. You should sing contemporary songs." Since the music executive and my friend had different tastes in music, the criticism and advice were not to be taken seriously.

If you and the other person do share a similar set of values, however, you should listen carefully and consider the advice and suggestions. Then put the criticism to work to help you overcome obstacles on the way to achieving your midterm and long-term goals.

Is the criticism too general?

Critical generalizations, such as, "This is lousy," or, "How stupid," or, "I don't like it," rarely provide much insight, whereas an examination of facts can be helpful. For example, if your boss says, "This doesn't work. Fit it!" but offers no specific feedback, you can ask,

"What exactly do you mean?"

"Can you give me a specific example?"

If the criticism is specific and insightful, listen and consider it carefully. Then use the criticism to help you get the results you need to achieve your goals.

Strategies to Help You Benefit from Criticism

"I love criticism, as long as it is unqualified praise."
—Noël Coward (1899–1973),
English actor, dramatist, and composer

Criticism is like a sharp knife. In the proper hands it can trim, slice, and pare food or a block of wood until it is just right. In the wrong hands, however, it can do severe damage. Follow these five strategies and you will deal with criticism in a way that maintains your self-esteem and motivation.

Five Strategies
That Elicit Constructive Criticism

Strategy 1: Listen for constructive criticism

Strategy 2: Ask for clarification and examples

Strategy 3: Ask for additional criticism

Strategy 4: Ask for suggestions and advice

Strategy 5: Tell people you value their comments

STRATEGY ONE:
LISTEN FOR CONSTRUCTIVE CRITICISM

Constructive criticism can help you achieve your goals if you know how to listen for it. When someone disapproves of your actions, it's natural to bristle, defend, explain, or justify your actions or decisions. Usually, this knee-jerk reaction only decreases your receptivity and may inhibit open communication between you and the other person. As a result, you may miss the opportunity to profit from his unique perspective. You can use criticism to facilitate your progress if you listen for valid points such as:

 Ideas you hadn't thought of yourself

Issues or details you may have overlooked

☆ Mistakes you can correct

☆ Answers you need, but have been unable to find

☆ Alternate viewpoints, solutions, and problem-solving strategies

☆ Specific ways to improve what you do

STRATEGY TWO:
ASK FOR CLARIFICATION AND EXAMPLES

Critical people can help you achieve your goals if they can articulate what you did wrong or how you can improve. Unfortunately, a great deal of criticism, particularly in the workplace, is too general to be of much use. Take for example the impatient supervisor who chides a worker, "This will never do," or, "Do I have to explain everything to you?" Vague criticism such as this provides little information that anyone could use to get the job done right. You can elicit more specific feedback from a critical person by asking such questions as:

"What *exactly* did I do wrong?"

"Can you give me an example of what didn't work for you?"

"What part of the proposal is inadequate?"

"What specifically don't you like about it?"

"Is there a particular reason you don't care for this?"

"I really want to make this better. The more specific you are about how I can improve it, the more it will help me."

STRATEGY THREE:
ASK FOR ADDITIONAL CRITICISM

Asking for *more* criticism may sound crazy. However, it can help you achieve your goals more quickly by uncovering hidden problems or issues that others may be reluctant to bring up. For example, an art director criticized an eager assistant designer's layout for an advertisement. The assistant designer, assuming that there was only one problem, changed the layout based on that one criticism and brought it back to the art director. Then the director criticized the assistant designer's choice of type. Surprised and disheartened, she changed the typeface and returned it to the director, who saw something else he disapproved of. So the pattern continued until the art director finally assigned the project to another designer.

If the assistant designer had asked the art director for more criticism, she might have uncovered his other objections and saved both of them time, money, and frustration. By asking for more criticism, you can speed your progress toward your midterm and long-term goals. Use these examples to ask for more criticism:

"What else don't you like?"

"In what other ways do you want this changed?"

"Is there anything else you want me to fix?"

"Do you have any other reservations about . . . ?"

"Is there anything else you want to discuss before I continue?"

STRATEGY FOUR:
ASK FOR SUGGESTIONS AND ADVICE

Why not take advantage of a person's opinions and experience to help you achieve your goals? Granted, you might get an earful, but that's okay because you can choose what applies to you and your situation. This strategy is highly effective when addressing issues where you need additional problem-solving options. To elicit specific suggestions, ask specific questions. For example:

"How would you have handled the situation?"

"What would you do to correct the problem?"

"What would you suggest as my next step?"

"What would you do if you were in my position?"

STRATEGY FIVE:
TELL PEOPLE YOU VALUE THEIR COMMENTS

When someone offers you constructive criticism, tell her that you appreciate her input. By letting others know that you welcome useful comments and suggestions, they will be more likely to help you in the future. Let's face it: Most of us can use all the help we can get! Here are some ways to show that you value someone's input:

"I really appreciate you taking the time to look over and comment on my work."

"Please tell me anything that you think will improve what I do."

"Will you give me some feedback again?"

"Your suggestions have helped me achieve what I set out to do."

Successful People Gladly Listen to and Use Criticism

"He who can take advice is sometimes superior to him who can give it."
—Karl Ludwig von Knebel (1744–1834),
German poet and tutor to Prince Constantine

After you hear a critical comment, you have a decision to make: You can either accept, reject, or take more time to consider the critic's opinion. In the end, it is up to you to decide how to use the criticism. When you consider criticism carefully, it shows that you are goal-oriented and determined to succeed. Successful people know how to listen to and use criticism to achieve their goals. They also know that the ability to learn from others is one of the greatest resources available to anyone who wants to fulfill their dreams.

LITTLE EXERCISES THAT GET BIG RESULTS

Number Ten:
Turning Criticism
into Progress

Problem-Solving Strategy:
Defining Possible Solutions

*This strategy helps you use constructive criticism
to find solutions.*

What's the problem? Even constructive criticism can sap your enthusiasm and motivation to achieve your dreams if you do not attempt to find solutions. By suggesting possible options on how to deal with specific problems or issues, you'll use criticism to overcome hurdles between you and your dreams.

What to do: First identify a midterm goal that you have had trouble achieving. Then list two constructive criticisms that have prevented you from achieving this goal. Finally, list at least two possible solutions for each criticism that may help you achieve the goal.

Midterm goal: _____

Constructive
Criticism 1
_____
_____
_____

Possible
Solutions
_____
_____
_____

Constructive
Criticism 2
_____
_____
_____

Possible
Solutions
_____
_____
_____

FOLLOW-UP

Now that you know how to use criticism to help you tackle a tough midterm goal, refer to the exercises at the end of chapters five and six. Use this strategy to help you accomplish other stubborn midterm goals or steps. Look to see how you can modify other solutions to address other criticism. When you find the solutions to constructive criticism, they will help you achieve your goals.

Little Things Checklist

Listening to criticism isn't always pleasant, but it can help you achieve your goals. Here are some additional tips to help you use constructive criticism to get what you want.

- ✔ Look for opportunities to elicit constructive criticism from people whose opinions you value.

- ✔ Discuss your ideas, obstacles, and solutions with people whom you think can give you constructive criticism.

- ✔ Take constructive criticism and use it immediately to overcome obstacles and speed your progress toward your goals.

- ✔ Attempt to understand the reasoning behind constructive comments.

- ✔ Take special note when you hear the same criticism repeated by different people.

- ✔ Don't be offended if someone offers you unsolicited constructive criticism—just put it to good use.

WHAT'S NEXT?

Since you know how to listen to criticism and put it to work, you are ready to go on to chapter eleven. Your next step is dealing with . . . er . . . ah . . . can we do this tomorrow?

11

Twenty-One Jump Starts
for Procrastinators

"I won't think of it now. . . . I'll think of it all tomorrow, at Tara. I
can stand it then. . . . After all, tomorrow is another day."
—from *Gone with the Wind,*
by Margaret Mitchell (1900–1949), American author

ARE YOU LIKE Scarlett O'Hara and other people who put
things off until tomorrow? Do you get sidetracked from
your primary goals by dozens of small, low-priority tasks? Do
you frequently wait for the perfect time to do things . . . and
then miss opportunities? Do you avoid dealing with difficult
issues with the hope that they will go away? Do you ignore
minor problems until they turn into full-blown predicaments
that demand your immediate attention? If this sounds like you,
then you are not alone; millions of people describe themselves as
procrastinators. The good news is that with some self-discipline
and jump-starting strategies, you can kick this paralyzing habit
and achieve your dreams.

When Postponing Action Becomes a Habit, It's Time to Act

"The chains of habit are too weak to be felt until they are too strong to be broken."
—Samuel Johnson (1709–1784),
English lexicographer, critic, and poet

Mark Twain knew procrastinators would appreciate his jest when he said, "Never put off until tomorrow what you can do the day after tomorrow." If putting things off frequently leads to big problems and missed opportunities, then it is time to make some changes. People procrastinate for different reasons, but fear is a common denominator. The most common fears are of:

◆ Failing to achieve a goal

◆ Failing to meet others' expectations

◆ Being criticized

◆ Being rejected

◆ Making difficult changes

◆ Making mistakes

◆ Making commitments

◆ Taking risks

You can break a procrastination habit if you overcome such fears as these. You also need to look at your daily behavior to see if you are a *high-energy* or *low-energy* procrastinator. Once

161

you identify how you procrastinate, then you can adopt a strategy to break the pattern and get back to work.

High-Energy Procrastinators

High-energy procrastinators bounce like a ball from activity to activity, but rarely focus their efforts on the most important tasks. Their frenetic behavior keeps them busy, but a short attention span and lack of priorities prevent them from making any significant headway toward their goals.

There are three basic types of high-energy procrastinators:

The Neatnik   *The Rambler*   *The Dilettante*

NEATNIKS SPEND
TOO MUCH TIME ORGANIZING

"Neat people who go about furiously tidying things appall me; the neatest places I know are museums, stuffed with dead things."
—St. John Ervine (1883–1971),
Irish playwright and novelist

Neatniks spend more time and energy cleaning and organizing than working. They feel uncomfortable if anything is out of place and say that they need to have order around them before they can take action. Neatniks claim that they can really get going on a project once they organize everything.

However, they often fail to start because they don't want to make a mess or have to clean up their mistakes. Neatniks usually say that they can't do little bits here and there, but need to totally immerse themselves in their work. This all-or-nothing approach yields few results because Neatniks can always find something else that needs cleaning or organizing before they get down to work.

I know an artist who is also a classic Neatnik. She spends half the morning sharpening her colored pencils, cleaning paintbrushes, and rearranging tubes of paints on the table before she puts one dollop of color onto a canvas. By the time she is ready to paint, it's nearly lunchtime. She doesn't want to make a mess and then have to clean up again. So, it makes perfect sense to put off starting any painting until after lunch. After lunch, she makes a few telephone calls, runs an errand, and tidies up some drawer or closet. By the time three o'clock rolls around, she rationalizes that it's too late to get started, and she doesn't want to make a mess. So another day passes without painting. My friend's compulsion for order prevents her from reaching her long-term goal of selling her paintings in a local gallery.

RAMBLERS FOCUS
ON LOW-PRIORITY ACTIVITIES

"Gentlemen, you are now going out to play football against Harvard. Never again in your whole life will you do anything so important."
—Tad Jones (1887–1957),
Yale University football coach

Ramblers usually focus their prime time and effort on low-priority activities. They get things done, but what they accomplish does little to help them achieve their goals. For instance,

Ramblers procrastinate by watering the plants, baking a cake, walking the dog, chatting with the neighbors, talking on the telephone, or doing just about anything—except working on a specific goal-oriented activity. While Ramblers' energy may be high, their attention flits from task to task. They frequently start and stop activities, rarely maintaining their focus long enough to complete even modest midterm goals.

DILETTANTES LACK COMMITMENT TO LONG-TERM GOALS

"I can't imagine a person becoming a success who doesn't give this game of life everything he's got."
—Walter Cronkite (b. 1916),
American journalist and broadcaster

Dilettantes are procrastinators who do not commit to a long-term goal. They dabble in a variety of endeavors, but rarely finish what they start or reach a proficient or professional level in anything. They would rather play at one thing until they become bored. Then the Dilettante quits that effort and sets off on another, often totally different, course of action.

Dilettantes in business, for example, spontaneously dive into one entrepreneurial venture after another. Their great bursts of activity and enthusiasm go on until they reach an obstacle, or they lose interest. Then, it is as if someone punched a hole in a balloon. As the Dilettante's energy and confidence deflate, his progress slows, he procrastinates more, and eventually quits. When another new opportunity comes along that he can jump into, the Dilettante repeats the pattern of high-energy activity followed by disillusionment and abandonment of the goal. While Dilettantes often work very hard for short periods, they usually do not accomplish enough midterm goals to turn their dream into a reality.

I know a fellow who is a musical Dilettante. When I first met him, he was taking singing lessons because he wanted to be an opera singer. After a year or so, he decided that learning an instrument would help improve his voice, so he bought an expensive guitar. He took lessons and practiced hard for about three months and then gave it up. Next, he became passionate about the piano, so he invested several thousand dollars in a professional electric keyboard. After a while, he gave up that endeavor, too. Like all Dilettantes, he failed to focus his efforts long enough on one goal to accomplish little more than mastering the basics.

Strategies for High-Energy Procrastinators

STRATEGY ONE: MAKE A SCHEDULE AND STICK TO IT

If you are a Neatnik, a Rambler, or a Dilettante, you can accomplish a great deal by setting time limits for completing specific activities. Start by setting a time limit on organization and clean-up time. Then schedule, start, and finish specific goal-oriented activities. Soon you'll see progress where there once was only order. For example, a morning schedule for an artist who is a Neatnik might look like this:

Morning Painting Schedule

Total painting time: 3 hours, 15 minutes

Total organizing and clean-up time: 30 minutes

Total break time: 15 minutes

8:30–8:45 A.M.: Organize art supplies, review schedule

8:45–10:30 A.M.: Start painting

10:30–10:45 A.M.: Break

10:45 A.M.–12:15 P.M.: Continue painting

12:15–12:30 P.M.: Clean up for lunch

STRATEGY TWO:
ESTABLISH A DAILY ROUTINE
AND KEEP A LOG OF YOUR TIME

Establishing a daily work routine and keeping a log of the time devoted to a goal is an effective way for high-energy procrastinators to focus their efforts. If you are a Neatnik, the task of setting up a daily work log will be easy because it fits into your orderly approach to things. If you are a Neatnik, Rambler, or Dilettante, your challenge is to focus your efforts long enough each day on the correct tasks so you can fill in the chart. Use a notebook or calendar to record your total work time, including hours and even minutes. (Those minutes really add up!) You can also include your activities and what you accomplished each day. Totaling your time at the end of each day and week as if you were punching a clock reinforces your established routine. Moreover, seeing daily progress will give you the motivation you need to keep going toward your goal.

STRATEGY THREE:
COMPROMISE WITH YOURSELF
ABOUT HOW YOU DEFINE "ORDER"

Ramblers, Dilettantes, and Neatniks in particular focus too much on creating and maintaining order and not enough on specific midterm goal-oriented activities. To help break this procrastination pattern, redefine what constitutes an acceptable level of neatness and order. For example, if your goal is to repair your back porch, you don't need to clean the basement first. However, organizing your tools and materials would be helpful before you start the project. Keep in mind that when you redefine your sense of order, you simply redirect your focus to activities that relate more directly to specific tasks and goals.

STRATEGY FOUR:
GIVE YOURSELF PERMISSION
TO MAKE A MISTAKE (AND MAKE A MESS)

Most Neatniks, Ramblers, and Dilettantes fear making mistakes. Ironically, many important discoveries and successes came about as result of a so-called mistake. For example, during an experiment in 1839, inventor Charles Goodyear accidentally spilled a mixture of sulfur-rubber onto a hot stove. The result of this smelly and smoky mess was vulcanized rubber and the birth of a billion-dollar industry. R. Buckminster Fuller, the inventor of the geodesic dome, believed that he never learned from his successes, but only from his mistakes.

You can overcome the fear of making mistakes if you adopt George Bernard Shaw's philosophy: "A life spent making mistakes is not only more honorable but more useful than a life spent doing nothing."

STRATEGY FIVE:
FOCUS ON PRIORITY ACTIVITIES
THAT LEAD TO YOUR MIDTERM GOALS

If you are a Neatnik, Rambler, or Dilettante, you probably have difficulty focusing on priority tasks that relate directly to your specific midterm and long-term goals. To solve this problem, revisit the long-term goal, midterm goals, and flowchart of little steps that you identified in the exercises at the end of chapter one, chapter five, and chapter six. These are the priorities that you must focus on and complete if you are to achieve your dreams. Resist the impulse to divert your attention to low-priority tasks. Remember that the key to success lies in zeroing in and completing *important* details.

STRATEGY SIX:
CHOOSE *ONE* EASY PRIORITY TASK
AND COMPLETE IT

Choose one priority step or task from your flowchart that you estimate will take less than an hour to complete. Then attack the task head-on. Don't stop, leave your work area, or even look out the window until the hour is up or you have completed the task. You may want to use a timer to help you know when your time is up. If you do not complete the task within the hour, that's okay. Take a five-minute stretch break, reset the timer for another hour, and go back to work and finish the task.

STRATEGY SEVEN:
DOUBLE YOUR ESTIMATES
OF THE TIME TO COMPLETE TASKS

I used to become impatient when I didn't finish things quickly. Finally I learned that most everything—and I mean *everything*—took at least twice as long to complete as I anticipated. By doubling the time you estimate to complete the task, you will be mentally prepared to focus on the job until you have finished or the time is up. If you complete the task sooner, then you can take a break or go onto the next priority task. Be sure to give yourself more time to complete the step if you need it.

STRATEGY EIGHT:
ELIMINATE EXTERNAL
AND INTERNAL DISTRACTIONS

Neatniks, Ramblers, and Dilettantes are particularly vulnerable to distractions. The good news is that you can easily eliminate external distractions such as telephones or televisions. Eliminating such internal distractions as worrying about a family member or dealing with recurring health problems is more difficult. One successful method of coping with an internal distraction while you work is to visualize putting the problem into a box and sealing it shut. You can also imagine placing the sealed box with your problems inside into a closet and then closing the door. This visualization technique helps to temporarily eliminate internal distractions and allows you to concentrate and complete the important steps that lead to your goals.

STRATEGY NINE:
TAKE SHORT, TIMED BREAKS

Once you begin your project, don't work for hours on end. You need to take a few breaks, but only for specific lengths of time. Plan fifteen-minute breaks with longer lunch or dinner breaks—and stick to your schedule. You can set an alarm clock or use a timer to tell you when to get back to work. While some procrastinators may balk at this regimented approach, Neatniks, Ramblers, and Dilettantes are usually more productive when they work in a structured environment.

STRATEGY TEN:
MAKE A COMMITMENT
TO FINISH A SHORT PROJECT

If you are a Neatnik, Rambler, or Dilettante, you can start kicking the procrastination habit if you commit to seeing a short project through from beginning to end. The idea behind this strategy is to finish what you start and not to focus or worry too much about the outcome. Once you see yourself complete a short project, you will be more confident that you can finish longer and more challenging tasks.

STRATEGY ELEVEN:
DEFINE WHAT CONSTITUTES "FINISHED"

Neatniks, Ramblers, and Dilettantes often start working on projects without defining a specific goal or outcome. As a result, when they become tired, bored, or frustrated, they start procrastinating and ultimately give up. To overcome this obstacle, specifically define what it is you want to accomplish. By defining what constitutes "finished" *before* you start working, you'll know when you can go onto another task or new goal.

STRATEGY TWELVE:
FINISH ONE PROJECT
BEFORE STARTING SOMETHING NEW

Make it a habit to complete one task or goal before starting the next. This simple strategy helps you retain your focus and build your self-discipline. Apply this strategy to even the smallest tasks or steps. Soon you'll find that you are getting more things done and don't have to go back and tie up a dozen loose ends.

STRATEGY THIRTEEN:
CHOOSE YOUR NEXT ACTIVITY
FROM YOUR LIST OF MIDTERM GOALS

Most high-energy procrastinators make impulsive decisions instead of focusing on a predetermined set of goals. Therefore, carefully decide which activity to do next *before* you start it. Look at your long-term goals and review the billboards of midterm goals and the flowcharts of little steps you identified in earlier chapters. Choosing from these lists of your goals and priorities will keep you from getting sidetracked and will move you closer to your long-term goals.

STRATEGY FOURTEEN:
COMMIT TO A GOAL
FOR A SPECIFIC LENGTH OF TIME

Committing to work on a goal for a specific length of time will help you overcome the urge to jump ship and start something new. By persevering through the less exciting or difficult periods, you will continue to invest the energy and enthusiasm necessary to achieve your goals.

If you are a Neatnik, Rambler or Dilettante, try focusing your efforts on specific goals and outcomes, and you will accomplish more than you ever believed possible.

Low-Energy Procrastinators

Low-energy procrastinators take so long to begin, move at such a slow pace, and are so cautious that they often give up on their dreams before they get to the first midterm goal.

There are two main types of low-energy procrastinators:

The Thinker   *The Fantasizer*

"THINKERS" ARE OVERSENSITIVE TO MISTAKES

"If you would create something, you must do something."

—Johann Wolfgang von Goethe (1749–1832),
German poet and dramatist

Thinkers are low-energy procrastinators who spend too much time contemplating, pondering, and reflecting rather than getting down to business and doing something productive. While Thinkers may be creative, like most procrastinators they are oversensitive to criticism and the opinions of others. When inspiration fails to appear, negative self-talk often convinces the Thinker that the activity, task, or goal is probably pointless anyway.

"FANTASIZERS" AVOID RISK-TAKING

"Security is mostly a superstition. . . . Avoiding danger is no safer in the long run than outright exposure. Life is either a daring adventure or nothing."

—Helen Keller (1880–1968),
American writer, and lecturer on the sight- and hearing-impaired

Fantasizers are low-energy procrastinators who think big, but usually fail to invest even the minimum amount of energy required to accomplish the most basic goals. Typically they are so afraid of mistakes, criticism, or failure that they become overwhelmed by even modest projects. Fantasizers often blame other people or circumstances beyond their control for their lack of progress. Most Fantasizers do not take enough risks to achieve even modest goals.

Strategies for
Low-Energy Procrastinators

STRATEGY FIFTEEN:
BEGIN A SHORT, ENJOYABLE ACTIVITY
THAT RELATES TO A MIDTERM GOAL

If you are a Thinker or Fantasizer, you need to take action—any action. Write a silly story, build a bookcase, bake a cake, or learn a new song on the guitar. Just choose an enjoyable task or activity that relates to a midterm goal and have some fun. Don't worry if you make a mess or the results aren't great. What is important is to break the pattern of inertia. For example, a technique that novelists use to overcome writer's block is to write anything—a poem, limerick, love letter, whatever—just so they put words on the page. Eventually the lock on the novelist's imagination opens, and she can return to the original writing project.

STRATEGY SIXTEEN:
BEGIN WITH THIRTY-MINUTE BLOCKS
OF UNINTERRUPTED WORK TIME
NO MATTER HOW YOU FEEL

As a Thinker or Fantasizer you can overcome procrastination by taking action before your inner voice says, "I don't feel like doing it right now." Instead of avoiding the task, work a specific amount of time *even if* you don't feel inspired. Usually, given a little time and activity, the logjam breaks and your creative juices will start flowing. For example, focus on an easy task that takes about thirty minutes to complete. When you finish, ask yourself, "What can I do next?"

Thinkers and Fantasizers need to establish a working routine that focuses on small successes. When you complete easy tasks that take about a half hour, your momentum and confidence will increase. When you pick a task, concentrate on it for the entire block of time. See how good a job you can do, but don't strive for perfection. If it takes you less than thirty minutes to finish the task, look at what you've done and see if you can make any improvements. The object of this strategy is to *finish the task* and do the best job you can in the allotted time.

STRATEGY SEVENTEEN:
RESERVE JUDGMENT FOR LATER

If you are a Thinker or Fantasizer, it is deadly to criticize your efforts while working on a specific task. Being too judgmental can stifle your creativity, deplete your confidence, and discourage you to the point of stopping all activity. Do not fall into this old procrastination trap. One way to avoid this pitfall is to suspend judgment of the task or activity until much later. For example, many successful artists, writers, musicians, and other "creative types" find it necessary to wait for days or weeks after completing a project before objectively evaluating it. You can do the same thing by saying to yourself, "I'll get started, see what I can accomplish, and reserve judgment for later."

STRATEGY EIGHTEEN:
FOCUS MORE ON THE PROCESS
AND LESS ON THE OUTCOME

Most low-energy procrastinators are oversensitive to criticism and failure. When you worry less about what you produce and concentrate more on the process itself, you will begin to see results. Of course, some efforts will be more satisfactory than others, but as most achievers are quick to point out, both success and failure lead to completing goals. Once you accept that mistakes are okay, you will learn how to profit from all your efforts and achieve your goals. Desensitize yourself to mistakes by keeping this proverb in mind: "He who makes no mistakes, makes nothing."

STRATEGY NINETEEN:
KEEP FOCUSED ON THE BIG THINGS,
BUT DO THE LITTLE THINGS

If you are a Thinker or Fantasizer, then you probably daydream about doing great things, and that is a positive trait. Our world is a better place because of dreamers like Thomas Edison, Albert Einstein, Helen Keller, and Mary McLeod Bethune. These successful people knew how to turn their dreams into reality. They understood the value of visualizing their success and working on the details that led to achieving their specific goals. You can take the first step to overcoming procrastination if you agree to start and finish small tasks that relate to your big dreams. To help keep your attention focused on the big things, visualize yourself doing different little tasks that lead to your midterm goals. Then see yourself enjoying the benefits of achieving your long-term goal.

STRATEGY TWENTY:
ESTABLISH A REGULAR TIME
AND PLACE TO WORK EVERY DAY

Ignacy Jan Paderewski, the Polish composer and pianist, was known for the many hours he practiced every day. After one impressive concert, Queen Victoria called him a genius. Wanting the Queen to know that his virtuosity was really the result of unrelenting practice, Paderewski said, "Perhaps, Your Majesty, but before that I was a drudge."

If you find a consistent time and place in which to apply yourself to a series of smaller tasks, then you will begin to see results, too. Just break each task into small, manageable parts and consistently work on each one. You'll happily discover that when you link several smaller tasks, they will help you achieve your midterm and long-term goals. For example, let's say that you want to alphabetize all the records, cassettes, and CDs in your music collection. Start by taking twenty or thirty minutes to alphabetize the records, cassettes, and CDs whose performers' last name begins with the letters *A* through *H*. The next day, alphabetize the CDs whose performers' last name begins with the letter *I* through *R*. Continue this process until you have alphabetized your entire collection.

STRATEGY TWENTY-ONE:
REWARD YOURSELF AFTER COMPLETING
AN UNINTERRUPTED BLOCK OF WORK TIME

Low-energy procrastinators need to focus first on the process, then on results. Once you overcome your inertia, you can slowly but steadily improve your productivity. Give yourself a simple reward at the end of an uninterrupted work session. Perhaps it's a short walk, a small snack, or a ten-minute guitar session. Do not choose any rewards that will interfere with your ability or desire to begin the next task. Only claim your reward when you've logged your time or completed the job. Continue this process with each new task you accomplish.

If you are a Thinker or Fantasizer, take small risks and don't worry about the outcome. You'll see that you too can turn pipe dreams into results.

If You Take Action
You Can Overcome Procrastination

"A man would do nothing if he waited until he could do it so well that no one could find fault."
—Cardinal John Henry Newman (1801–1890),
English theologian

If you are a high-energy or low-energy procrastinator, you can achieve success by eliminating your habit of putting things off until later. Changing old patterns of behavior is rarely easy and probably won't happen overnight, but with concerted effort and self-discipline you can achieve remarkable goals. So, if you are a Neatnik, Rambler, Dilettante, Thinker, or Fantasizer you know what to do now. Use these twenty-one jump starts, and you'll turn "I'll think about it tomorrow" into "There's no time like the present."

LITTLE EXERCISES THAT GET BIG RESULTS

Number Eleven:
Developing a
Productive Routine

Problem-Solving Strategy:
Making a Daily Schedule

This strategy helps you begin and sustain your efforts
from the first step through the last so you can achieve
your midterm and long-term goals.

What's the problem? Everyone puts things off from time to time, but if you are going to get what you want, then you'll need to consistently work toward your goals. Making a schedule shows the relationship between investing time and getting results.

What to do: The objective of this exercise is to build your self-discipline and improve your daily work habits. If you define your goal and specific tasks the day before, you'll be ready to go to work at "the bell." Complete the following schedule for one week and stick to it. (Change the times to fit your existing schedule.) Keep track of your total hours each week and you'll achieve more than you ever believed possible.

Monday Schedule

My goal this morning is to:

_____

_____

8:30 A.M.–8:45 A.M.: _____

8:45 A.M.–10:30 A.M.: _____

10:30 A.M.–10:45 A.M.: Break

10:45 A.M.–12:15 P.M.: _____

12:15 P.M.–12:30 P.M.: _____

What I achieved today:

_____

_____

_____

_____

FOLLOW-UP

Establishing consistent work habits helps you achieve your long-term goals. Your next step is to make a commitment to stick to your schedule. If you really want to kick the procrastination habit, read and sign this personal contract.

Contract to Kick
the Procrastination Habit

My long-term goal is:

_____

I agree to:

1. Make a schedule of tasks and stick to it the best I can.

2. Keep a log of the time and activities I devote to achieving my goals.

3. Allow myself the opportunity to make mistakes.

4. Start goal-oriented tasks instead of low-priority activities.

5. Finish one project before I start something new.

6. Keep pursuing my goals even if I get bored, discouraged, or distracted.

7. Reserve judgment about the results of my efforts until later.

8. Keep working to achieve my dreams without giving up.

Signed _____

Date _____

Little Things Checklist

Overcoming procrastination takes persistence, self-discipline, and a "do it now" attitude. The following tips will help you stay on the path to your long-term goals.

- ✔ Remember that procrastination is a habit that you can overcome, thirty minutes at a time.

- ✔ List all unfinished tasks or projects and rank them based on how they help you achieve your midterm and long-term goals.

- ✔ Work to finish projects that are closest to completion and that help you achieve your midterm and long-term goals.

- ✔ Resist the temptation to jump to another project or task before you finish what you started.

- ✔ Make lists of tasks and check off each as you complete them.

- ✔ Look to see what other projects you can finish before you begin something new.

- ✔ After a month or so, review your list of finished and unfinished projects. Then pat yourself on the back and give yourself a reward—you are kicking the procrastination habit.

WHAT'S NEXT?

Now that you know how to get the little things done without getting sidetracked, you can go on to chapter twelve. Your next step is how to do a great, but not perfect, job.

12

Managing Perfectionism
to Get Things Done

"Have no fear of perfection—you'll never reach it."
—Salvador Dalí (1904–1989), Spanish surrealist painter

THE GERMAN CONDUCTOR Otto Klemperer was as well known for his musical sensitivity as he was for his severely exacting technique. He was by all accounts a perfectionist who rarely seemed pleased with even the most accomplished efforts and was very sparing with praise. After one particularly good performance, he smiled with approval and congratulated the orchestra with an enthusiastic, "Good!" Surprised by the compliment, the musicians applauded, to which Klemperer replied, "Not that good."

Perfectionism Can Prevent You
from Achieving Your Dreams

Perfectionists expect nothing less than the very best from themselves and the people they work with. As a result, their exceptionally high standards and expectations can lead to great accomplishments. Sometimes, however, being a perfectionist can also get in the way of achieving your goals and enjoying success. Do you refine and redo a task so many times that you never finish what you start? Do you set your standards so high that no matter how good a job you do, the results never quite satisfy you? Does the fear of making a mistake keep you from going on to the next step of a project?

Five Strategies
to Manage Perfectionism

If perfectionism prevents you from achieving your midterm and long-term goals, use the following strategies to see how much more you can accomplish while you maintain your high standards.

Strategy 1: Set reasonable expectations for yourself

Strategy 2: Focus on and complete your top priorities first

Strategy 3: Set a maximum time limit to complete each task

Strategy 4: Remain focused on "the big picture" while attending to details

Strategy 5: Know when to say, "I'm ready for the next step"

STRATEGY ONE:
SET REASONABLE EXPECTATIONS
FOR YOURSELF

"This became a credo of mine—attempt the impossible in order to improve your work."

—Bette Davis (1908–1989),

American actress

The French Impressionist artist Paul Cézanne exemplifies a perfectionist who frequently set unreasonable expectations for himself and others. While painting the portrait of his friend and art dealer Ambroise Vollard, Cézanne insisted that the poor man pose at least 115 times. When someone asked Cézanne about the progress of the portrait, he said, "I am not entirely pleased with the shirt front."

Setting reasonable expectations doesn't mean that you must sacrifice your high standards, but it does require that you make some compromises. If you are a perfectionist, give yourself a break and avoid the trap of saying that anything short of "perfect" is unacceptable. You can still be a successful person, and strive for excellence, and achieve your goals without attaining perfection.

To set reasonable expectations, ask yourself:

"Short of perfection, what results will make me happy and help me achieve my midterm and long-term goals?"

"What level of excellence—short of perfection—do I need to accomplish to achieve my next midterm goal?"

"What is more important? Getting each detail perfect—which is impossible—or completing my midterm goal so I can accomplish my long-term goal?"

STRATEGY TWO:
FOCUS ON AND COMPLETE
YOUR TOP PRIORITIES FIRST

"Read all the best books first, or you may not have a chance to read them at all."
—Henry David Thoreau (1817–1862),
American essayist

Perfectionists need to keep focused on their top priorities or they can lose sight of what is most important. I knew an advertising executive who insisted on micromanaging every detail of a major promotion for a new client. Obsessed with doing a "perfect" job, she became immersed in the countless low-priority details of the project. Unfortunately, she failed to complete the budget (a high-priority task) on time and to the client's satisfaction. As a result, she lost the client's confidence and the advertising account.

Perfectionists typically get bogged down in minor details instead of making timely progress toward their goals. One way to avoid this pitfall is to delegate or ignore less important details so you can focus on and finish your priority tasks. To help you zero in on the most important tasks to accomplish, ask yourself:

What important tasks *must* I finish today?

Of these tasks, which *one* is my top priority?

What impact does this task have on my midterm or long-term goals?

You can make a simple chart to help you focus on top priorities. For example, let's say your goal is to turn your garage into a workshop. Here is how you could prioritize the tasks and achieve your goal. You'll have a chance to make your own top priorities chart in the exercise at the end of this chapter.

Top-Priority Tasks
- ❑ Repair concrete floor
- ❑ Build the workbench
- ❑ Rewire electricity
- ❑ Put in new lighting
- ❑ Install a pegboard for hanging tools
- ❑ Build shelves for building supplies

Lower-Priority Tasks
- ❑ Clean out old tools
- ❑ Sharpen tools
- ❑ Organize building supplies
- ❑ Alphabetize how-to-build books
- ❑ Paint tool shapes on the pegboard
- ❑ Label jars of screws and nails

By focusing on the top priorities, you will be achieving your goal of turning the garage into a workshop. After you complete the top priorities, you can focus on the lower priorities as you find the time.

STRATEGY THREE:
SET A MAXIMUM TIME LIMIT
TO COMPLETE EACH TASK

"Have you got a problem? Do what you can where you are with what you've got."
—Theodore Roosevelt (1858–1919),
twenty-sixth president of the United States

Perfectionists often ignore time limits when it comes to getting things done. I know a perfectionist who had a goal to clean out and organize the closets in her apartment in one weekend. To accomplish this goal, she needed to clean three closets each day.

By the end of Sunday, she had spent all her time cleaning and organizing only one closet, and it still wasn't "perfect."

Setting a time limit to complete specific midterm goals or tasks is one way for perfectionists to reach their long-term goals. If you are a perfectionist who spends too much time on tasks, here are some dos and don'ts to keep you moving closer to you goals:

- **Do** a test run and see how long one task takes to complete.

- **Don't** focus on irrelevant details at the expense of completing the total job.

- **Do** stick to the times you set to complete a task.

- **Don't** keep doing the same task repeatedly until it is "perfect."

- **Do** the best job you can within a certain length of time.

- **Don't** worry if every detail of the job you do isn't "perfect."

- **Do** remember that the job doesn't need to be done perfectly, but it must be done.

STRATEGY FOUR:
REMAIN FOCUSED ON THE BIG PICTURE
WHILE ATTENDING TO DETAILS

"Keep your eyes on the prize."
—from a traditional African-American folk song

Keeping the long-term goal clearly in sight is always a challenge for the perfectionist. Take my friend Fred, for example.

He was a hardworking entrepreneur who wanted to build a small business editing videos of weddings and birthdays. An admitted perfectionist, he would spend fifteen or more hours turning each home video into "perfect little television shows" for his clients. The problem was that he charged only $75 per job for his time, materials, and expertise. At that rate of return, Fred's hourly pay was about $5. This example shows how perfectionism can impede progress toward a long-term goal—in Fred's case, a profitable business.

Whether your dream is to change careers or paint your living room, if you focus only on the details without keeping your eyes on the big picture, you probably will not achieve your goal. To keep your long-term goal in sight, ask yourself:

Am I making acceptable progress on my midterm and long-term goals?

Am I getting bogged down in details?

Are the details that I am accomplishing leading me to my midterm and long-term goal?

STRATEGY FIVE:
KNOW WHEN TO SAY,
"I'M READY FOR THE NEXT STEP"

"Striving to better, oft we mar what's well."
—from *King Lear,* by William Shakespeare (1564–1616),
English dramatist and poet

Perfectionists have a difficult time saying "It's done." For example, have you ever finished a project, and then decided to add a final touch, which ruined the whole thing? If you are a perfectionist, your extremely high standards push you to do the best possible job you can, and that's great. However, if you don't know when to say "enough is enough," you may diminish what you have accomplished and not achieve your ultimate goals.

Perfectionists often use negative self-talk that prevents them from saying, "I'm done." If you find yourself using the negative self-talk of a perfectionist, then use the following examples to change it to the positive talk of a high achiever. That way you'll maintain your high standards and accomplish your goals.

Perfectionist's Negative Self-Talk	High Achiever's Positive Self-Talk
💣 "I just can't get it perfect!"	⭐ "I've finished the job and it meets my high standards."
💣 "I'll get this darn thing perfect if it kills me."	⭐ "I'm proud of the job I have done, even if it isn't perfect."
💣 "I can never do anything without making at least one tiny mistake."	⭐ "I've done my best to achieve my goal."
💣 "It's still not perfect."	⭐ "I'm done with this task and moving onto my next step."

Don't Let Unattainable Standards Stall Your Progress

"Even if you are on the right track, you'll get run over if you just sit there."

—Will Rogers (1879–1935),
American humorist

Working hard without making timely progress toward your goals is frustrating. That is why every perfectionist needs to learn how to set attainable self-expectations. At first, you may find it difficult to focus your efforts more on top-priority tasks than on superfluous details. At the same time, setting time limits for how long you spend working on your priorities will increase your productivity and propel you forward. When you keep focused on the big picture, you'll get things done, maintain your high standards, and know when to go on to the next step in your plan. The big message here is: Achieving your dreams and long-term goals is well within your grasp, *if* you don't let perfectionism stand in your way.

LITTLE EXERCISES THAT GET BIG RESULTS

Number Twelve:
What Are Your Top Priorities?

Problem-Solving Strategy:
Prioritizing Tasks

This strategy helps you overcome perfectionism
by focusing on the tasks
that are most important to tackle first.

What's the problem? How can a perfectionist stay focused and complete the most important tasks when facing a big job? One way is to rank the importance of all the tasks. Then focus on and complete *only* the tasks with a "top-priority" rating before you get bogged down in minor details.

What to do: The objective of this exercise is to sort and set your top priorities. First write your long-term goal. Then fill in the spaces to see what tasks you need to focus on first.

My long-term goal is:

_____

_____

_____

_____

_____

Top-Priority Tasks:

_____

_____

Lower-Priority Tasks:

_____

_____

FOLLOW-UP

Once you have identified your top priorities, then rank them according to importance.

Rank of My Top-Priority Tasks:

_____

_____

_____

_____

_____

_____

_____

You can take this exercise one step further by revisiting your midterm goals and little steps in chapters five and six. Repeat the first part of the exercise and prioritize all the steps and tasks. Then order your top priorities and complete them one by one. Remember, these tasks don't need to be done perfectly for you to achieve your long-term goals; they just need to be done.

Little Things Checklist

Perfectionism can be a curse if you let unrealistic expectations stand between you and your dreams. You can get what you are working for and maintain your high standards by following these tips:

✔ Make perfectionism work for you by setting high, yet attainable standards.

✔ Learn from perfectionists like Thomas Edison. When a friend asked him how he coped with so many failures, he said, "I didn't fail ten thousand times. I successfully eliminated, ten thousand times, materials and combinations which wouldn't work."

✔ Review your expectations before you start a task to make sure they are reasonable.

✔ Develop a learn-as-you-go approach so you can profit from your mistakes and do better the next time.

✔ Focus on the positive aspects of what you accomplish; not just what you did wrong.

✔ Don't let perfectionism become an excuse to avoid taking risks, failing, or making mistakes.

✔ You do not need to accomplish every step perfectly to be successful.

✔ Remember that you can always go back and make anything you do better after you have achieved all your top-priority tasks.

WHAT'S NEXT?

Now that you know how to manage your perfectionism, you are ready to go on to chapter thirteen. Your next step is to make those deadlines!

13

Setting and Meeting
Your Own Deadlines

*"If I could, I would stand on a busy corner, hat in hand, and beg
people to throw me all their wasted hours."*
—Bernard Berenson (1865–1959),
American art critic and historian

AFTER MARY KAY Ash's husband died, she took on the
total responsibility of starting a new cosmetic business
and raising three children. Mary Kay knew that in order to
meet her personal and professional deadlines, she had to make
each minute in the day count. Every night after she put the
kids to bed and the house was quiet, she listed the six most
important tasks she had to accomplish the next day. Using this
simple yet effective time-management technique helped her
create the hugely successful Mary Kay Cosmetics.

Meeting Self-Imposed Deadlines
Yields Results

Are you pursuing your midterm and long-term goals only
when you have some spare time? Do you rarely accomplish

your goals in the time that you set aside? When you do set a deadline, is it based on wishful thinking? Do you race against the clock because you underestimated how much time it takes to complete various tasks? As you get more deeply involved in a project, does it become painfully clear that you won't complete it on time? Even when you have plenty of time, do you frequently leave projects unfinished? Has wasting time become a bad habit that leaves you empty-handed at the end of the day? If you answered yes to any of these questions, then you need to learn how to set manageable deadlines and use your time more effectively.

Three Steps to Setting Self-Imposed Deadlines

Setting and meeting manageable deadlines comes with experience. The following steps will help you set your own deadlines so you can achieve your midterm and long-term goals.

Step 1: Specify what you want to accomplish

Step 2: Estimate how long each step will take to complete

Step 3: Commit to a specific day by which you want to complete your goal

---

STEP ONE:
SPECIFY WHAT YOU WANT TO ACCOMPLISH

"You have to know exactly what you want out of your career. If you want to be a star, you don't bother with other things."
—Marilyn Horne (b. 1934),
American opera singer

Whether your long-term goal is to become an actress or open a restaurant, to succeed you will need to set your own deadlines and manage your time wisely. In chapters five and six you learned how to set long-term and midterm goals, and how to break them down into small steps. Now is the time to define your specific objectives.

For example, when I taught the guitar, most students asked me how long it would take them to learn to play the instrument. However, before I could answer them, I needed to know their specific objectives. That's when I asked them *exactly* what they wanted to accomplish. Although all of the students wanted to learn how to play the guitar, many of their specific objectives differed. Their responses included:

◆ Strumming a few chords and singing easy songs

◆ Picking lead guitar solos in a rock and roll band

◆ Reading music to play jazz standards

◆ Playing and singing songs in the school's holiday program

◆ Learning one specific song for a role in a movie

Now I had some specific information I could use to estimate how long it could take each of them to achieve their respective goals. For example, I said it would take a few months of easy practice for the students who wanted to learn how to play and sing simple folk songs. I told the budding rock star it could take six months to a year of steady practice to master the skills needed to play lead guitar in a rock band. I told the actor he could learn "Blue Suede Shoes" in about a month, but only if he practiced every day for at least one hour. For the student who wanted to play jazz standards, I estimated that she would need to take weekly lessons for at least two years to accomplish her goal.

Clearly defining what you want to accomplish helps you focus your efforts and achieve what you want within a specific time. To define your objectives, ask yourself:

What *exactly* do I want to achieve?

What can I do after I achieve this goal that I cannot do now?

What should I do today that will enable me to accomplish my goals for tomorrow?

To make sure that this objective fits into your "big picture," ask yourself:

If I meet this objective, will it help me achieve my midterm or long-term goals?

What can I do today that will simplify accomplishing my objectives for next week? Next month? Next year?

You'll get a chance to define a specific objective in the exercise at the end of this chapter.

STEP TWO:
ESTIMATE HOW LONG EACH STEP
WILL TAKE TO COMPLETE

"Success often depends upon knowing how long it will take to succeed."

—Montesquieu (1689–1755),

French political philosopher

To set your own manageable deadlines, you'll need to know all the steps and estimate how long each will take to complete. Estimating correctly how long it takes to accomplish a task is a combination of guesswork and experience. The one thing I've discovered about setting deadlines is that almost every step of a process—no matter how big or small—usually takes two to three times longer to accomplish than I originally estimated. Therefore, I always double (or even triple) my estimate of how long a task takes to complete.

I also learned a valuable technique for setting deadlines from a topnotch managing editor who rarely missed a deadline. Her secret was what she called the "fudge factor." She would add 30 percent when estimating the cost, the time it would take, as well as other resources necessary to complete a project on time. The "fudge factor" saved her from missing deadlines more than once. For example, during a one-year publishing project, several computers broke down, people fell ill, clients changed their minds, and a host of other problems cropped up. If this savvy editor had not factored these unknowns into the schedule, we would have missed our deadlines and overspent the budget.

Here are some tips to improve your estimating skills:

◆ Be realistic when you consider how long it takes to complete tasks.

◆ Determine whether you will need help in completing the tasks (and if so, when, where, and how much).

◆ Confirm that your materials, equipment, and other logistics are available before making an estimate.

◆ In your estimates, factor in external factors such as family obligations, health issues, holidays, and even the weather.

◆ Know your personal and physical limitations when you estimate how long it will take you to complete a task.

◆ Don't forget to add in the "fudge factor" to your estimates.

You'll get a chance to estimate how long each step to achieve your objectives will take in the exercise at the end of this chapter.

STEP THREE:
COMMIT TO A SPECIFIC DAY BY WHICH
YOU WANT TO COMPLETE YOUR GOAL

"Better three hours too soon than a minute too late."
—from *The Merry Wives of Windsor,*
by William Shakespeare (1564–1616), English dramatist and poet

Now comes the tricky part: You must pinpoint an exact date or time to complete your objective. In other words, set a deadline. Is your projected deadline a day, week, month, or year away? Do you set the deadline, or is it someone else's decision? For example, if you are in the early stages of a job search and you want to update your résumé, then you have more flexibility determining your deadline. But what if a job opportunity pops up unexpectedly and a prospective employer wants you to fax a résumé and cover letter by the end of the day? Then your deadline is only a matter of hours away.

Many people fail to achieve their dreams because they do not set deadlines to complete their midterm and long-term goals. Once you establish *what* you want to accomplish, then make a commitment regarding *when* you want to accomplish it. Here is how to set a manageable deadline:

- ◆ Get a calendar and a colorful pen or marker.

- ◆ Review what you want to accomplish and your estimates of how long the tasks involved will take you to complete.

- ◆ Allow extra time for setbacks and unexpected delays.

- ◆ Pick a specific day to achieve the goal and then ask yourself: Is this deadline based on thoughtful evaluation? Is this deadline manageable? Can I achieve this deadline without killing myself?

- ◆ If the answer to all three questions is yes, then write the date on your calendar.

You'll get a chance to commit to a specific day that you want to complete your goal in the exercise at the end of this chapter.

Adjust Your Deadlines as You Progress, if Necessary

Once you have set your own deadline, your next step is to complete your tasks and goals within that period. As you get under way, you'll see how accurate your estimates are and whether you need to make some adjustments. Since many projects can take on lives of their own, be flexible and ready to add or subtract time as needed. For example, you might complete most of your midterm goals ahead of your deadline. If that happens, then you can speed up your efforts and achieve your long-term goal sooner than you originally estimated.

If, on the other hand, you have completed only one or two of your objectives and you have passed your midterm deadline, then you probably need to refocus on your top priorities or make some adjustments. Have you allotted a reasonable amount of time to complete your objectives, given your daily schedule and prior commitments? If the answer is no, then give yourself more time. If you have had enough time but did not achieve your objectives, then you may need to find other people to help you. (See chapter fourteen.) If you are like many people, however, you may need to improve your time management skills so you don't waste the time you have allotted to complete your goals.

Six Time Boosters to Help You Meet Your Deadlines

"One always has time enough, if one will apply it well."
—Johann Wolfgang von Goethe (1749–1832),
German poet and dramatist

Stanley Marcus, the department store executive of Neiman-Marcus, described time as "the most precious asset I have, and of which I have the least supply." While money, materials, and even opportunities come and go, there are only twenty-four hours in a day. Do you complain that you have too little time, yet waste much of this nonrenewable resource? Studies show that most high achievers are acutely aware of time and always attempt to use every moment they have to move even small steps closer to their goals. Therefore, if you adopt the same attitude and awareness of how you spend your time, you can achieve your goals, too. The following time boosters will improve your time management skills and help you meet your own deadlines.

Six Time Boosters

Time Booster 1: Make a master list with deadlines

Time Booster 2: Make a daily schedule to consistently meet your deadlines

Time Booster 3: Organize your work space

Time Booster 4: Do similar tasks at the same time

Time Booster 5: Find the right time and place for the task

Time Booster 6: Eliminate distractions

TIME BOOSTER ONE:
MAKE A MASTER LIST WITH DEADLINES

"Great moments in science: Einstein discovers that time is actually money."

—from *The Far Side,* by Gary Larson (b. 1950),
American cartoonist

Are your bulletin board, desk, and refrigerator filled with dozens of notes for all the unfinished tasks, projects, and telephone calls that require your attention? To simplify your life and get more done on time, consolidate these tasks with their deadlines onto one master list. This way you can see at a glance everything that needs to be done, and you can better plan your priorities. Using a master list prevents you from overlooking important details as you work toward meeting your deadlines. It also allows you to decide which tasks to do yourself and those that someone else can do for you. Take out a sheet of paper right now and write "Master List" across the top. Keep the list handy so you can add new tasks as they come up and subtract tasks as you complete them.

TIME BOOSTER TWO:
MAKE A DAILY SCHEDULE
TO CONSISTENTLY MEET YOUR DEADLINES

"He who every morning plans the transactions of the day, and follows out that plan, carries a thread which will guide him through the maze of the labyrinth of the most busy life."

—Hugh Blair (1718–1800),
Scottish clergyman

Consistency and success go together. Take for example, the winning strategy of John Madden, the former head coach of the Oakland Raiders football team. He looked to his players for solid play every time rather than a big play occasionally. He believed that consistent performance was the key to winning football games. I emphasized the same point during a recent writing workshop after one participant mentioned that she didn't have enough time to write. To prove that most of us waste time, I gave each student a daily schedule divided into half-hour sections. The task was for them to list their typical daily activities in the half-hour blocks of time from 7:00 A.M. to 10:00 P.M. Their goal was to find at least two empty blocks of time—between thirty to sixty minutes each day—in which they could *consistently* devote to writing their books. Many participants were surprised at how much time they really had at their disposal to meet their deadlines. One woman told me that this exercise helped her discover the time she could consistently use to write an audiotape to sell at her workshops.

Make a daily schedule of your tasks by referring to your master list. As you complete the tasks that lead to your goals each day, you'll make your self-imposed deadlines. Here are three ways to make a daily schedule:

- ◆ Buy a "day runner"–type organizer at your stationery store and use the preprinted sections to organize each day of the week.

- ◆ Get a three-ring binder with lined paper. Use each line as a half-hour block of available time and fill in the activities you want to accomplish for each day.

- ◆ On an oversized calendar, make appointments with yourself to complete the work necessary to consistently meet your deadlines.

TIME BOOSTER THREE:
ORGANIZE YOUR WORK SPACE

"A place for everything and everything in its place."
—Samuel Smiles (1812–1904),
Scottish social reformer and author

Nothing wastes time and interferes with goals more than lost papers, misplaced files, missing books, or broken tools. Being organized makes every deadline easier to meet. Rather than let chaos ruin your chances for success, take time at the beginning of a project to get organized. Let's hope you won't need to spend weeks getting ready, but a little time well spent organizing your work space, materials, tools, and resources can pay you back down the road. For example, if you want to better manage the time you spend in your home office you can:

◆ Clean your work space

◆ Create a file for your ideas

◆ Consolidate storage areas

◆ Refurbish supplies

◆ Throw away outdated information

◆ Clean up computer files

◆ Prune your Rolodex

◆ Create a long-term schedule

◆ Pin your goals on a bulletin board

◆ List resources and materials you need

◆ Check out books from the library

◆ Order and alphabetize your bookshelf

TIME BOOSTER FOUR:
DO SIMILAR TASKS AT THE SAME TIME

"There can be no economy where there is no efficiency."
—Benjamin Disraeli (1804–1881),
English diplomat and prime minister

When you use your time efficiently, you will achieve your goals within a planned time frame. Look for similar tasks on your master list and complete them at the same time. Thinking ahead and combining similar tasks can save time and can help you become more productive. For instance, I know a couple who one summer set some ambitious home improvement goals. To get all the work done by their deadline (the first snowfall), they listed all the supplies required for each project. Then they bought everything they needed on sale in one trip to the building supply store. Not only did the couple save time, money, and effort (the store delivered most of the materials for free), but they had the necessary supplies when they needed them. Here are three easy ways to combine similar tasks in a home office to save time so you can meet your deadlines:

◆ Combine all your important telephone calls into one block of time.

◆ Open *all* your mail (discarding the junk) before reading or responding to each correspondence.

◆ Schedule back-to-back appointments. (Note: Be sure to give yourself a comfortable cushion between appointments if you or the other person is running a little late.)

TIME BOOSTER FIVE:
FIND THE RIGHT TIME
AND PLACE FOR THE TASK

"Dost thou love life? Then do not squander time, for that's the stuff life is made of."

—Benjamin Franklin (1706–1790),

American statesman, inventor, author

Some high achievers get the most done in unexpected places and at unusual times. Consider Ann Landers, for example. For nearly forty years, she wrote her daily newspaper columns and answered her mail while soaking in the bathtub every evening after her family had gone to bed. I know several professional speakers who make sales calls only from 8:30 A.M. to 11:30 A.M., and then write and practice their speeches in the afternoons. For my part, writing in the morning and editing in the afternoon is the most productive use of my time. If I write or edit too much after 9:00 P.M., my work will have more than the usual number of mistakes. On the other hand, a writer friend of mine does her best work between the hours of midnight and 4:00 A.M. To discover when and where you do your best work, ask yourself:

At what time of the day or night am I most productive?

When do I have the fewest distractions?

When am I most alert and efficient?

Although you may need to experiment to find when you are most productive, when you do find your best hours, you'll save time, accomplish more, and meet your deadlines.

TIME BOOSTER SIX:
ELIMINATE DISTRACTIONS

"A distraction is to avoid the consciousness of the passage of time."
—Gertrude Stein (1874–1946),
American writer

It's amazing how at the end of the day you wonder where all the time went and what you accomplished. Frequent interruptions, telephone calls, unexpected visitors, or even a computer game can rob you of precious time that you can never get back.

My computer came loaded with the card game "solitaire." While I am not your classic computer game player, I decided to try it and found it fun. Soon I was playing a game of solitaire every day before I started my workday. Then I began playing a game after lunch before I returned to writing. Soon I was stopping my work for a "solitaire break." The games usually took only five minutes or less to play, but I began to see a big problem. At this rate, I would spend over an hour a week, five hours a month, or the equivalent of about sixty hours a year playing solitaire during my most productive work time. That had to stop if I wanted to meet the deadlines and goals I had set for myself. By eliminating this one distraction, I recaptured valuable time that I would have lost if I had continued playing the game. The following tips will help eliminate one of the most common distractions—the telephone:

- ◆ Use a telephone answering machine to take calls during your most productive work times.

- ◆ Have a timer handy to limit how long you chat.

- ◆ Tell friends a convenient time to call you.

♦ Tell telemarketers that their call has caught you at a bad time and that you cannot talk—even for a minute.

♦ Develop a few friendly lines to end your telephone conversations or to say that you will call back later. For example:

> "Sorry to cut you short, but need to finish what I'm doing by . . ."

> "It's been great chatting, but I've got to get back to what I was doing."

> "I'd love to hear more about . . . , but I'm afraid I need to get back to work."

> "I'm sorry I can't talk now. Can I call you back later this afternoon?"

> "I'm on a deadline. Can I give you a call tomorrow?"

Make Your Own Deadlines and You'll Achieve Your Dreams

"Take care of the minutes, and the hours will take care of themselves."
—Philip Dormer Stanhope, 4th Earl of Chesterfield (1694–1773),
English statesman, orator, and author

President John F. Kennedy was fond of telling a story about the great French colonial administrator Louis Lyautey to illustrate the value of timely action. It seems that one day Marshal Lyautey asked his gardener to plant a particular kind of tree outside his office window. The gardener objected, citing that the species was slow-growing and would take nearly one hundred years to reach maturity. "In that case," Lyautey ordered, "there is no time to lose. Plant it this afternoon."

It's satisfying to see yourself getting things done and making progress toward your midterm and long-term goals. That's what setting and making your own deadlines is all about. When you follow the three steps for setting manageable deadlines and use the time boosters to get more done, your big dream will soon become a reality.

LITTLE EXERCISES THAT GET BIG RESULTS
Number Thirteen:
Creating Your Own Deadline

Problem-Solving Strategy:
Setting a Deadline

This strategy helps you accomplish a specific objective within a specified time.

What's the problem? Without self-imposed deadlines, you probably will not commit enough focused time and effort to accomplish all the necessary steps that lead to your midterm and long-term goals. By setting and meeting self-imposed deadlines, you can achieve your dreams on schedule.

What to do: The objective of this exercise is to set a self-imposed and manageable deadline for one midterm goal. First choose one midterm goal from the exercise at the end of chapter five. Next, write the steps and the estimated time to complete each step. Then set a manageable deadline. Finally, sign your name and commit to meeting your deadline.

Deadline: _____

Midterm goal: _____

Today's date: _____ Deadline: _____

Steps to accomplish:

1. _____
2. _____
3. _____
4. _____
5. _____
6. _____

Estimated hours/days to complete each step:

1. _____
2. _____
3. _____
4. _____
5. _____
6. _____

Total: _____

I agree to work my hardest to meet this self-imposed deadline.

Signed: _____

FOLLOW-UP

After you set your deadline, attach it to your bulletin board or in a place where you can see it every day so that it will never be out of your sight—or mind. Keep track of your progress to see if your time estimates are reasonable. Then adjust your deadline as necessary. You can take this exercise to the next step by creating deadlines for each of your midterm goals and each of the little steps that you defined in chapters five and six.

Little Things Checklist

Setting and meeting self-imposed deadlines takes experience and self-discipline. The following tips will help you meet your deadlines so you can accomplish your midterm and long-term goals.

✔ Set realistic objectives that you can accomplish in a specific amount of time and you will meet your deadlines.

✔ Define your specific objectives as clearly as possible, as well as the time you think it will take to complete each objective.

✔ Review your daily schedule to find unused half-hour blocks of time that you can devote to meeting your deadlines.

✔ Include extra time into your schedule so you can double-check for errors and add a "touch of polish" to your work.

✔ If you have underestimated how much time or resources it will take to complete a task, look for help or revise your deadline.

✔ If you frequently waste time looking for lost items, reorganize your work space.

✔ When you miss a deadline, reassess the tasks, set a new due date, and get back to work.

✔ When you meet a self-imposed deadline, celebrate and give yourself an appropriate reward.

WHAT'S NEXT?

Now that you know how to set and meet your own deadlines, you're ready to go on to chapter fourteen. Your next step is finding people who can help you.

14

Finding Help
in All the Right Places

"I surround myself with quality people who make me look good."
—Dennis Conner (b. 1943),
sailboat skipper, winner of America's Cup

IS YOUR GOAL of a dream vacation, house, new career, or pet project fading away because you can't personally do everything that needs to be done? Do you miss critical deadlines because you are overwhelmed with countless details? When it comes to the unpleasant tasks, do you put them off or do a poor job? Are you faced with vital steps that you lack the expertise to complete? If you answered yes to any of these questions, then you probably need some help in accomplishing your goals and keeping your dream alive.

Asking for help to achieve your dreams is not a sign of weakness. On the contrary, most successful people admit that they do not achieve their goals strictly through their own efforts, but have received help from a variety of sources. High achievers usually give much of the credit for their success to their staff, spouses, coaches, coworkers, mentors, teachers, and even their competitors.

You Need the Right Help to Get the Job Done Right

"You can't build a reputation on what you are going to do."
—Henry Ford (1863–1947),
American automobile manufacturer

If you feel overwhelmed by some tasks or steps you need to accomplish, then consider reaching out to skilled people. When you get help with tasks you can't or don't want to do yourself, you can focus on what you enjoy most and do best. Instead of burning out and quitting, you'll make your deadlines, complete your projects, and reach your ultimate goals.

Two Steps to Getting the Right Help

Step 1: Assessing your needs

Step 2: Finding the right people

STEP ONE:
ASSESSING YOUR NEEDS

"You seldom accomplish very much by yourself. You must get the assistance of others."
—Henry Kaiser (1882–1967),
American industrialist

Before you look for help in achieving your goals, make a "wish list" of skilled people whose assistance you could use.

What skills do you need to progress to the next level that you currently do not possess? Which hurdles must you clear to meet your next deadline or objective? Which obstacles stand between you and your goals that seem insurmountable? If money were no object, what tasks would you like others to do for you?

For example, if you are self-employed and want to expand your business, your wish list might look like this:

◆ A designer to create new promotional materials

◆ An efficiency expert to organize your office

◆ An accountant to keep the books and prepare your tax return

◆ A computer coach to teach you new software programs

◆ An office assistant to update your mailing list and fill orders

◆ A sales person to prospect for new customers

If you are planning on attending college, your wish list might look like this:

◆ A career counselor to help you select your major

◆ A tutor to help you prepare for your college entrance exam

◆ A fellow student who can recommend the best classes and instructors

◆ A professor who can help you find a work-study job on campus

◆   A speech trainer who can help you prepare for your entrance interview

◆   An athletic coach who can help you apply for an athletic scholarship

Once you define your needs, then you can look for the right people who can help you fulfill them.

STEP TWO:
FINDING THE RIGHT PEOPLE

"I'm not the smartest fellow in the world, but I can sure pick smart colleagues."
>   —Franklin Delano Roosevelt (1882–1945),
>   thirty-second president of the United States

Whether your dream is to sail around the world or to create your own computer software company, finding the right people to help you achieve your goals requires patience, good communication skills, a willingness to take some risks, and a little luck. In addition, you won't know for sure how it will work out with someone until you start the process. Even if you find a good candidate, it likely will take time and effort to iron out the wrinkles and create a smooth working relationship. The following dos and don'ts will help you avoid some pitfalls when deciding whether to seek someone's assistance.

Do seek people who:

☆   Have a proven track record in the kind of expertise you're seeking. (There are plenty of people who will promise you anything to get your business. Conduct an informal interview and check references before you make any commitments.)

☆ Take the time to understand your specific needs. (The people who will help you the most are those who are willing to listen the most.)

☆ Demonstrate high personal standards and ethics. (If someone promises you a way to achieve your dream that sounds too good to be true, it probably is.)

☆ Can work independently and in a group. (Building a team of skilled and cooperative people will help you achieve your goals more quickly and with better results.)

☆ Are high achievers. (The people who will help you the most are the ones who know what it takes to succeed.)

Don't expect people to:

💣 Volunteer all their time and services to your cause. (Although some people may offer some assistance for free, you probably will need to pay for or barter for most of the help you get.)

💣 Make decisions for you. (How can anyone help you achieve your goals if you don't know what they are?)

💣 Help you at the expense of themselves or others. (Your goal is probably not a top priority for anyone other than yourself, except for a spouse or family member.)

💣 Produce good results without providing them with input, feedback, and encouragement. (Be prepared to invest time and energy in the people from whom you seek help.)

YOU CAN FIND THE RIGHT PEOPLE
IN MANY DIFFERENT PLACES

"The strong individual is the one who asks for help when he needs it."
—Rona Barrett (b. 1938),
American columnist and television personality

When a newspaper reporter asked Willie Sutton, a famous robber, why he held up banks, Sutton replied, "That's where the money is." This thief had lousy ethics but insightful reasoning. Whether you are looking for people to help you build an adventure playground or plan a cross-country bus tour, finding resources is easier when you know where to look for them. If you need people to help you achieve your goals, you'll find them in places such as these:

◆ Classified newspaper advertisements for help around your home

◆ Clubs, social organizations, and religious groups for volunteers

◆ Directories of professionals

◆ Employment agencies for professional office help

◆ Friends or employers who will write reference letters for you

◆ Independent contractors for help with remodeling

◆ Libraries, schools, and parks for free programs and services

◆ Local high schools or colleges for apprentices and interns to help in your business

- Mentor programs for business advice

- Networking groups for more professional contacts

- Peers who are willing to share their expertise

- Professional associations for seminars to upgrade your skills

- Referrals from people who do what you want to do

- Resources from the backs of books related to your goal or interest

- Telephone book yellow pages for anything or anyone you need

Let's Take a Closer Look at Finding a Mentor

"You're going to have times when you're going to wish you had some-one to talk to—someone to get you through some of those trying times."

—Hank Aaron (b. 1934),
American baseball player
with the most lifetime home runs

Mentors are people who volunteer their time, experience, and effort to help others fulfill their potential and achieve their goals. Different from teachers, coaches, tutors, partners, or counselors, a mentor's role is more that of a one-on-one facilitator. There are three common forms of mentoring: short-term, informal, and long-term.

SHORT-TERM MENTORS

"Good advice has no price."
—proverb

Powerful advice on how to handle a specific situation is an example of short-term mentoring. Your mentor's guidance helps you deal with a short-term problem and might include a personal story of how he or she handled a similar situation. For example, my first day as an elementary school substitute teacher was so hectic that by 10:30 A.M. I wasn't sure I would make it to lunchtime without tying the students to their chairs or quitting. Fortunately, during the morning recess break, an experienced teacher offered some valuable advice. "I plan every minute of the day," she said, "so the kids don't have time to give me any trouble." My short-term mentor helped me survive that day and taught me one of the most important rules in teaching: Be prepared.

INFORMAL MENTORS

"In those days he was wiser than he is now—he used frequently to take my advice."
—Winston Churchill (1874–1965),
British statesman and prime minister

Getting occasional advice that helps guide you to your midterm and long-term goals is an example of informal mentoring. In this situation, you can draw on your mentor's knowledge and experience to help you achieve your various objectives. For example, after I joined the National Speakers

Association, one friendly member offered me his advice and experience. He told me, "Don, if you ever want to ask me anything about the speaking business, just let me know." Over the years, I have called him every so often with questions or ideas, and he shares his knowledge and experience with me. As an informal mentor, he has helped me achieve several of my professional speaking goals.

LONG-TERM MENTORS

"It is the province of knowledge to speak and it is the privilege of wisdom to listen."
—Oliver Wendell Holmes (1809–1894),
American physician and author

Finally, you may need help from a mentor over a longer period. Clergyman and author Dr. Norman Vincent Peale often told the story of how he found his long-term mentor, Robert Rowbottom. One day after attending church, the two men were talking and Peale revealed some personal doubts about his own abilities as a minister. Rowbottom told him, "Listen son, and never forget it. Never build a case against yourself." With those encouraging words, Norman Vincent Peale found a long-term mentor to whom he looked to for advice for more than fifty years.

Where to Find a Mentor

You can find a mentor to help you achieve your dreams in organizations related to your area of interest. Many associations, social organizations, and business groups sponsor mentor programs for their members. For example, as a member of the

National Speakers Association, I have been a mentor for several speakers who dream of writing and publishing a book. Organized programs usually offer a more systematic approach and focus on achieving specific goals.

Joining an organization isn't the only way to find a mentor. Perhaps you admire and want to model yourself after someone. You could write a short letter to introduce yourself and ask if he would consider becoming your mentor on an informal basis. You never know and might get a positive response. Another place to find a mentor is through the religious associations and volunteer groups. Many of their members enjoy serving as mentors to people who seek advice. Whether you are seeking a short-term, informal, or long-term mentor, keep the following points in mind:

- Always thank the mentor for her assistance.

- Never take advantage of a mentor's goodwill by asking for too much time.

- In most cases, avoid discussing with your mentor matters of too personal a nature.

- See mentors as role models and facilitators, not someone to whom you complain.

- Do not expect a mentor to make decisions for you.

- Maintain your independence with your mentor.

MENTORS RATE A "10" FROM SOME OF AMERICA'S MOST SUCCESSFUL PEOPLE

In his book, *The Achievement Factors,* B. Eugene Griessman asked successful authors, athletes, businesspeople, and entertainers how important mentors were in achieving their goals. On a scale of 0 (low) to 10 (high), Hank Aaron, Mary Kay Ash, Malcolm Forbes, Kris Kristofferson, Janet Leigh, Stanley Marcus, Sandra Day O'Connor, and Normal Vincent Peale gave their mentors a "10." If mentors helped these successful people achieve their goals, then a mentor can probably do the same for you.

LITTLE EXERCISES THAT GET BIG RESULTS

Number Fourteen: "Who You Gonna Call?"

Problem-Solving Strategy: Using Outside Resources

This strategy focuses on seeking information, expertise, and assistance from various sources to help you find solutions.

What's the problem? You don't always have all the information, know-how, or time you need to overcome the obstacles between you and your long-term goals. By using outside resources, you can focus on what you do best and obtain the help you need to achieve your dreams.

What to do: The objective of this exercise is to identify practical outside resources to help you complete specific tasks. First decide on the tasks you need help with to achieve your goals. Then match the tasks with the sources of information and people listed or any other outside resources you can think of.

INFORMATION RESOURCES

- almanacs ◆ annual reports ◆ biographies ◆ databases
- dictionaries ◆ encyclopedias ◆ Internet and online ser-

vices ◆ libraries ◆ magazines ◆ newspapers ◆ professional directories ◆ telephone books ◆ trade journals ◆ trivia books

HUMAN RESOURCES

◆ business associates ◆ coaches ◆ contractors ◆ consultants ◆ counselors ◆ coworkers ◆ employment agencies ◆ family ◆ friends ◆ fraternal organizations ◆ mentors ◆ networking groups ◆ peers ◆ professional associations ◆ religious groups ◆ social organizations ◆ teachers ◆ tutors ◆ veterans groups ◆ volunteer organizations

Tasks that I need help to complete that can help:	Outside resources that can help:
1. _____	1. _____
2. _____	2. _____
3. _____	3. _____
4. _____	4. _____

FOLLOW-UP

Now you know where to find the outside resources that can help you achieve your goals. Your next step is to decide which task or problem to focus on first. Choose one midterm goal that is easy to complete. Then find the right information or people to help you. Once you accomplish this goal, then progress to the more complicated midterm goals that require additional time, effort, skill, and outside resources to complete.

Little Things Checklist

Although no one said that accomplishing your dream was going to be easy, the good news is that there are plenty of people who can help you along the way. Use the following tips to find the right people who will help you achieve your goals.

- ✔ Whenever possible, use referrals to find the people you need to help you.

- ✔ Help others achieve their goals, and they will do the same for you.

- ✔ If a person can't help you accomplish your goals, then ask if he knows someone else who can.

- ✔ Surround yourself with the best people you can find.

- ✔ Don't expect anyone to work harder than you to help you succeed.

- ✔ Always thank people for their efforts on your behalf, even if they do not get results.

WHAT'S NEXT?

Now that you know where to find the right people to help you achieve your goals, you're ready to go on to chapter fifteen. Your next step is to cross the finish line!

15

Crossing
the Finish Line

"Always bear in mind that your own resolution to succeed is more important than any other thing."

—Abraham Lincoln (1809–1865),
sixteenth president of the United States

MANY PEOPLE CONSIDER Abraham Lincoln the savior of the United States. When he was inaugurated as president in 1861, his long-term goals were to stop the spread of slavery and to preserve the American Union in case the southern states' secessions led to war. "The Great Liberator" accomplished both his dreams. His will to succeed earned him the reputation as one of the greatest men of all time, and, unfortunately, cost him his life. While Lincoln is considered a success by any standard, you may not know about his many failures. Here are just a few of the many hardships and setbacks that he overcame to win the nation's highest office:

- Abraham Lincoln was born into a poor family and his parents were virtually illiterate.

- His education was sporadic and limited.

◆ Lincoln failed in business at the ages of 22 and 24.

◆ He had a nervous breakdown at the age of 27.

◆ Lincoln was defeated in eight different elections, including runs for the Illinois legislature, the U.S. Senate, House of Representatives, speaker, elector, and vice president.

◆ Even when Lincoln was president, he constantly struggled to achieve his dream of "a government of the people, by the people, and for the people."

The moral of this story is, never give up—no matter how many failures, hardships, or successes you experience. As you approach the finish line of your long-term goal, you will need to persevere and follow through on your game plan if you are to succeed. Plus, once you achieve your dream, you will need to consider some other critical issues. Whether you want to become an Olympic athlete, build a house, or run for political office, use these five reminders before and after you complete your goal.

Five Reminders Before and After You Cross the Finish Line

Reminder 1: Persevere until you achieve your goal

Reminder 2: Expect realistic rewards

Reminder 3: Acknowledge those who helped you

Reminder 4: Attend to your personal relationships

Reminder 5: Maintain a modest demeanor

Reminder One:
Persevere Until
You Achieve Your Goal

"There is no mistake so great as the mistake of not going on."
—William Blake (1757–1827),
English poet, artist, and mystic

In 1985, after a record-setting rookie season, the twenty-one-year-old pitcher Dwight Gooden received the Cy Young Award and launched a professional baseball career that most athletes dream of. However, Gooden's remarkable ascent would not last. By the early 1990s, recurring drug and money problems plagued his career. As his losses on the mound increased, he was traded from club to club. It didn't take long for his once storybook career to lay shattered, nearly in ruins. Many fans considered Gooden's career washed up. However, in 1996 George Steinbrenner, the owner of the New York Yankees, decided to give Gooden another chance. After spending two seasons without pitching a game, on May 15, 1996, Gooden surprised everyone (including himself) by tossing a no-hit game against the Seattle Mariners in Yankee Stadium. Fans, players, coaches, and well-wishers cheered wildly and praised his remarkable achievement. The key to Dwight Gooden's accomplishment was that he persevered in his goal to get the final out of the game and make a successful comeback to his baseball career.

The impulse to give up or lose your focus on your goal can happen anywhere along the way, but you may be particularly vulnerable as you near the end of your project. As for me, when I am about a month away from finishing a book writing project, I can get tired and distracted. Therefore, I need to concentrate even harder to stay focused and finish the job with the best possible results. Here is what you can do to hang in there until you cross the finish line:

◆ Say to yourself something like, "Stay focused on the tasks at hand. Only three more weeks (or however long) and I'll be finished."

◆ Mark the days off on your calendar as you get closer to completing your goal.

◆ Remind yourself that the job doesn't need to be perfect, but it needs to be finished.

◆ If you slow down or stop, draw on your reserves and keep going.

◆ Tell yourself that you can rest *after* you have completed your goal.

◆ Don't accept *any* excuse to quit—no matter how much you might want to.

◆ Remind yourself of the benefits of achieving your goal.

Reminder Two:
Expect Realistic Rewards

"Don't pin much hope on the mail, and when the phone rings don't expect anyone wonderful to be calling."
—Andy Rooney (b. 1919),
television commentator, humorist, and author

Congratulations! You've finally published the great American novel that took you three years to write. You crack open the bottle of champagne, drink a toast with your friends, and sit back and wait for the big royalty checks. You are absolutely positive that movie contracts, speaking engagements, and celebrity endorsements will start rolling in any minute. Well, don't hold your breath. Perhaps you *will* be the next Stephen King, but the cold fact is that more than 50,000 books are published each year, and bookstores often return slow sellers to the publishers after only a month or two on the shelves. Although some authors do get rich by writing a book, a more realistic expectation might be a modest increase in business, income, or recognition in your particular field.

The moral of this story is that just because you achieved your long-term goal, it does not mean that you are automatically entitled to receive unlimited wealth and opportunity, or assured future success, without additional effort. Hopefully, the benefits you derive from your efforts will justify the energy and investment you've made. But keep things in perspective, for if your unrealistic expectations go unfulfilled, your motivation to complete other projects may suffer.

HOW TO AVOID
UNREALISTIC EXPECTATIONS

When you succeed at something, it's natural to dream about all the wonderful things that will happen for you. If, however, you find that you are frequently disappointed with the real benefits you gain, then consider the following suggestions:

◆   Discuss your expectations with others who have achieved similar goals.

◆ Don't assume that everyone will be as happy about your success as you are.

◆ Just because you achieved a goal, don't expect people to beat a path to your door.

◆ Keep your expectations realistic and in perspective.

Reminder Three:
Acknowledge Those
Who Helped You

"When a man tells you he got rich through hard work, ask him, 'Whose?'"
—Don Marquis (1878–1937),
American novelist and humorist

Some people become so preoccupied with their own achievements that they may forget who helped them along the way. An author friend of mine failed to mention her literary agent's name in her book's acknowledgments. The agent was justifiably disappointed and upset, especially since selling my friend's book and negotiating her contract took considerable time and effort. Omissions such as these, while they may seem small, can dampen others' willingness to help you in your future endeavors.

WHAT TO DO IF YOU NEGLECTED
TO ACKNOWLEDGE THE HELP OF OTHERS

Getting caught up in our own goals can lead to some oversights. If you failed to acknowledge the help of others, you can make up for your negligence by:

- Writing the person a thank-you note acknowledging your appreciation for their help.

- Sending a small gift, such as flowers, or an invitation to lunch or dinner.

- Offering to reciprocate in any way you can.

- Recognizing their contribution to your success with a toast at your next get-together.

- Telling colleagues or friends about how she helped you succeed.

Reminder Four: Attend to Your Personal Relationships

"If you bungle raising your children, I don't think whatever else you do well matters very much."
—Jacqueline Kennedy Onassis (1929–1994),
First Lady, wife of President John F. Kennedy,
book editor

Achieving difficult long-term goals often requires sacrifices from the people you care about the most. To neglect or ignore your personal relationships for too long—even for a good cause—can have a negative impact on your marriage, family, and friendships. Avoid paying an unnecessarily high price by balancing your needs with those of your family and friends.

WHAT TO DO IF YOU ARE NEGLECTING YOUR PERSONAL RELATIONSHIPS

Your relationship with family and friends can suffer if you do not spend time with them regularly. To reverse this trend and to keep your personal relationships healthy and thriving, you can:

- Recognize the importance of balancing work and family.

- Apologize for past inconsiderate behavior.

- Schedule regular times on your calendar to be with your family and friends.

- Mark special days such as anniversaries and birthdays in red ink on your calendar so you don't overlook them.

- Plan some special events to make up for previously canceled time together.

- Make it a rule not to cancel time set aside for family or friends.

Reminder Five: Maintain a Modest Demeanor

"I am the greatest!"
—Muhammad Ali (b. 1942),
American boxer and first to win
three world heavyweight titles

Your own achievements may impress you, but take care how you express this opinion to others. If you exaggerate your accomplishments or expect special treatment, you may leave a negative impression on others. Of course, some famous people have elevated boasting and self-promotion to an art form. Take Muhammad Ali, for instance. Once, while waiting to take off in an airplane, the flight attendant asked him to please fasten his seat belt. In a playful voice Ali responded, "Superman don't need no seat belt." The flight attendant didn't miss a beat when she said, "Superman don't need no airplane, either."

WHAT TO DO IF YOU BLOW YOUR OWN HORN A LITTLE TOO LOUDLY

I'll never forget the day when I sold my first writing assignment—an audio script about healthy snacking for children. As I walked down the streets of New York I felt as if I were on top of the world. What a feeling! I was on cloud nine. After about a week of congratulating myself, a close friend said, "Don, come back down to Earth with the rest of us." At first, his remark offended me. Then I realized that my friend had given me some valuable advice: It's a great feeling when you achieve a goal after working hard, but don't let it go to your head.

Whether you graduated from medical school or passed your driver's test, it's okay to pat yourself on the back when you achieve your dream, but don't let your achievements overwhelm you. Here are a few dos and don'ts to help you maintain a modest demeanor:

☆ **Do** remember that most people find humility more appealing than conceit.

💣 **Don't** ask for too many special privileges.

240

☆ **Do** resist inflating your achievements.

💣 **Don't** overreact to criticism.

☆ **Do** abstain from making pretentious statements about what you have accomplished.

💣 **Don't** get upset if your achievement does not impress others.

☆ **Do** talk about topics other than you or your accomplishments. (You may have heard about the actress at the cocktail party who said, "I've talked enough about myself, so let me ask you a question. What do you think of my new film?")

Keeping Your Achievement in Perspective

"You will go far, but be sure to come back."
—proverb found inside a Chinese fortune cookie

Now that you have achieved your big dream, it's time to pause for a moment. You've spent a lot of time and energy focusing on and accomplishing the little things, and you've done a great job. You have succeeded in your quest because you finished what you started. You are enjoying the fruits of your labor because you had reasonable expectations from the beginning. Your friends, family, and peers share in your happiness because you have remained modest and thanked them for their help and support. By using these reminders before and after you cross the finish line, you are keeping your eyes on the big picture and setting the stage for your next big goal.

241

LITTLE EXERCISES THAT GET BIG RESULTS

Number Fifteen:
What Have I Forgotten?

Problem-Solving Strategy:
Checking Key Issues

*This strategy helps you address five important issues
before and after you achieve your goal.*

What's the problem? It's easy to get so wrapped up in achieving your goals that you may have overlooked some important issues. By using the five reminders presented in this chapter, you can address these matters before and after you cross the finish line.

What to do: The objective of this exercise is to uncover any omissions in five critical areas. Write two ways you can use each reminder.

REMINDER ONE:
WHAT CAN I DO TO PERSEVERE
UNTIL I COMPLETE MY LONG-TERM GOAL?

_____

_____

_____

_____

REMINDER TWO:
WHAT ARE MY REASONABLE EXPECTATIONS
AFTER I ACHIEVE MY GOAL?

_____

_____

_____

_____

REMINDER THREE:
WHO HAS HELPED ME ACHIEVE
THE LITTLE THINGS
AND MY MIDTERM AND LONG-TERM GOALS?

_____

_____

_____

_____

REMINDER FOUR:
WHAT SPECIAL THINGS CAN I DO
FOR THE PEOPLE I CARE MOST ABOUT?

_____

_____

_____

_____

REMINDER FIVE:
WHAT CAN I DO TO MAINTAIN
A MODEST DEMEANOR,
EVEN THOUGH I'M THRILLED
THAT I ACHIEVED MY GOAL?

_____

_____

_____

_____

FOLLOW-UP

Imagine that someone asked you to present a toast at an awards banquet in your honor. What would you say to the audience about what you have accomplished? Write a short toast or letter praising yourself and pin it on your bulletin board or somewhere you can see it. Then treat yourself to a reward of your choice—you deserve it!

Little Things Checklist

Achieving a long-term goal is one of the best feelings in the world. The following little things will help you know what to do next.

✔ Take care not to rest on your laurels.

✔ Sharpen any rusty skills so you are ready to take on a more challenging goal.

✔ Dust off some old ideas that never got developed.

✔ Brainstorm new ideas for another project related to your past success.

✔ Complete an unfinished project.

✔ Look to see what other people in your field or area of interest are doing.

✔ Rework a failed endeavor and see if you can achieve results.

WHAT YOU'VE LEARNED IN STEP FOUR

In Step Four you have learned that when it comes to achieving your goals, perseverance is more important than talent, luck, money, or anything else. Many successful people consider perseverance their secret to success. One of those people was Albert Einstein. The story goes that one day Einstein needed a paper clip for the pages of a recently completed research article. He and his assistant searched his office, but the only paper clip they could find was one that was severely bent out of shape. Undaunted, Einstein figured he could straighten the paper clip if he had the right tool, so the two men expanded their search for an implement to do the job. After more searching, the assistant discovered an entire box of paper clips stuffed away in a drawer and concluded that they solved the problem. However, to the assistant's surprise, Einstein took a new paper clip and shaped it into a tool to straighten the bent paper clip. The puzzled young man asked why he didn't just use a new paper clip for his article. Einstein answered, "Once I am set on a goal, it becomes difficult to deflect me."

Perseverance is unquestionably one key factor to achieving goals. In this section, you learned how to persevere by taking advantage of criticism and not letting negative people undermine your desire to succeed. Now that you have adopted a "do it now" strategy, procrastination won't sap your confidence or drive. Doing the job right means setting and achieving attainable goals and then forging on to the next step, even if what you have done isn't "perfect." You have learned that making a deadline is easy if you create a reasonable schedule for yourself and stick to it. Now you know that you don't need to do everything alone. People are often happy to help you accomplish your goals—all you need to do is look in the right place and ask them for their assistance. Finally, you know five important issues to address before and after you have achieved your long-term goal.

WHAT'S NEXT?

Now that you have achieved your dream, you are ready to go on to "Step Five, Build on Your Success" and chapter sixteen. Your next step is learning from what you accomplished.

Step Five

BUILD ON YOUR SUCCESS

"Press on: Nothing in the world can take the place of perseverance. Talent will not; nothing is more common than unsuccessful men with talent. Genius will not; unrewarded genius is almost a proverb. Education will not; the world is full of educated derelicts. Persistence and determination alone are omnipotent."

—Calvin Coolidge (1872–1933),
thirtieth president of the United States

16

You've Achieved Your Dream, So What's Next?

"If God would give me some clear sign! Like making a large deposit in my name at a Swiss bank.
—Woody Allen (b. 1935),
American film director, actor, and author

C AN YOU IMAGINE getting up at six every morning and putting your body through three grueling hours of pain, day after day, month after month, for nearly eleven years— motivated only by the goal of competing in the Olympic games? Bill Carlucci, the winner the bronze medal at the 1996 Olympics in rowing, did just that in pursuit of his dream. Like most athletes who competed in the games, Bill received only fleeting fame and scant financial reward. Therefore, the truest measure of his success was the fact that he achieved his lifelong goal to win an Olympic medal.

Celebrate Your Success

"Success to me is having ten honeydew melons and eating only the top half of each one."
—Barbra Streisand (b. 1942), American singer and actress

Once You Have Achieved
a Long-Term Goal You Can:

☆ *Celebrate your success*

☆ *Evaluate what you achieved*

☆ *Pursue your other dreams*

Whether your dream was to earn a college degree, patent an invention, or win a chess competition, now is the time to reward yourself for achieving a difficult objective. Sit back, enjoy the fruits of your labors, and reflect on what you have achieved. Basking in the glow of this golden moment and acknowledging that you have accomplished a long-term goal is an important part of success. Whatever you have achieved may not be perfect, but you can still take the credit you deserve and savor it. Because you have completed your long-term goal, you not only have the confidence and skills to fulfill other dreams, but you deserve a special reward. The following suggestions are just a few possible ways to treat yourself after you have achieved your long-term goal:

- Have a celebration party

- Buy yourself a special gift

- Take a week's vacation

- Sleep in late

- Take a friend to dinner

- Go to a spa and get a massage
- Relax and read a favorite book
- Pop a bottle of champagne

Although You Achieved Your Dream, Someone May Still Criticize You

"The play had only one fault. It was kind of lousy."
—James Thurber (1894–1961),
American cartoonist and writer

Liberace, a flamboyant pianist, was famous for his grand piano decorated with burning candles and his spectacular sequin-encrusted skintight suits. A well-loved performer, Liberace was no stranger to unflattering remarks from high-brow music critics. After playing a sold-out concert at New York's Madison Square Garden, a local music critic panned his performance. Liberace remarked that the man's comments hurt him deeply—so much, in fact, that he "cried all the way to the bank."

Although you have accomplished a difficult long-term goal, there may be at least one person who will try to belittle your achievement and rob you of your success. If that happens, keep these two points in mind. First, you achieved your dream, and that makes you a success in your own eyes. Don't let anyone take that accomplishment away from you. Second, many successful and talented people have been laughed at, ridiculed, put down, maligned, and panned. Therefore, if someone describes you with unflattering remarks such as "failure," "hack," or "mediocre," don't worry—you're in good company.

Books abound with stories highlighting the lives and achievements of famous athletes, businesspeople, politicians, and humanitarians who failed—in the eyes of others. The fact that these people never gave up or saw themselves as failures shows their confidence and motivation. Here are a few classic examples of successful people who, according to their critics, were failures—at least *before* they became famous.

A GREAT WRITER   In 1889, an editor from *The San Francisco Examiner* newspaper sent the English novelist, poet, and short story writer Rudyard Kipling a rejection letter stating, "I'm sorry Mr. Kipling, but you just don't know how to use the English language." Undaunted, Kipling continued to write, and received the Nobel prize for literature in 1907.

AN INSPIRING WOMAN   Eleanor Roosevelt, while revered by many, was also brutally criticized for her independent views on a variety of issues, including women's rights. This never stopped her from voicing her opinions and supporting causes she believed in, whether they were controversial or not. These words sum up her attitude: "No one can make you feel inferior without your consent."

A PROLIFIC SONGWRITER   When Robert Zimmerman was a teenager, his classmates booed him off the stage of a high school talent show in Duluth, Minnesota. No one in the audience seemed to think he had much ability, given his whiny voice and unusual songs of social protest and the disenfranchised. Undeterred, Zimmerman packed his guitar and harmonica and moved to New York City when he was nineteen years old. There he changed his name to Bob Dylan and went on to become one of America's best-known folk singers and one of the most influential songwriters of his generation.

A SMASH MUSICAL   *The Fantasticks* (1960), New York's longest-playing musical, did not start out as a box office smash. The early reviews were so bad that several financial backers wanted its producer, Lore Noto, to close the show after the first week. Tom Jones, who wrote the book and lyrics and also appeared in the opening night cast, heard a critic in the audience complain loudly, "What's this thing about?" Jones was so upset about the remark that he became sick to his stomach in a cab on his way home. Jones said, "I just got out of the cab and vomited my way through Central Park."

Determined to succeed, Lore Noto, Tom Jones, and the cast made some adjustments. As the reviews improved, so did the audience response. Three years later, the Sullivan Street Theater, an off-Broadway house with only 150 seats, sold out every night. It took five years before everyone agreed that the show was a hit. The show is still running today, nearly forty years later.

Don't Let a Critic
Rain on Your Parade

These high achievers did not allow the negative comments of others to prevent them from enjoying their success. Follow their example. After you have enjoyed your success and given yourself a suitable reward, then it is time to move forward. Your next step is to take an objective look at what you accomplished so you can learn and profit from your experience.

EVALUATE WHAT YOU ACHIEVED

"Anyone can win, unless there happens to be a second entry."
—George Ade (1866–1944),
American humorist and playwright

For some highly competitive people, winning is the only standard of achievement. Consider the advice that race car driver Richard Petty's mother gave him after his second-place finish in his first professional race. "You lost!" she said. "Richard, you don't have to run second to anybody!" From that day, Petty went on to win the Daytona 500 seven times and the National Association of Stock Car Auto Racing championship seven times. He was the first stock car driver to win a million dollars.

Three Questions
to Assess Your Achievement

You'll benefit the most from your accomplishment if you objectively evaluate it. Use the following questions to help you assess your achievement.

Question 1: Did you achieve your original long-term goal?

Question 2: Which tasks did you excel in and enjoy the most?

Question 3: What will you do differently while pursuing your next dream?

Most successful people admit that no matter how good a job they do, there is always room for improvement. This philosophy does not diminish what they have achieved, but instead propels them to success in their future endeavors.

QUESTION ONE:
DID YOU ACHIEVE YOUR
ORIGINAL LONG-TERM GOAL?

"Mother always told me my day was coming, but I never realized that I'd end up being the shortest knight of the year."

—Gordon Richards (1904–1986),
British championship jockey's response
when told that he was to be awarded a knighthood

This question focuses on whether or not you accomplished your long-term goal as you envisioned it. For instance, when Christopher Columbus first set out from Palos, Spain, on August 3, 1492, his original goal was to discover a short route to the Indies. He was motivated by money and expected to become rich. His "great idea" was to sail 2,400 nautical miles west to a small group of islands near Japan. There he planned to establish an east-west trading company and become ruler of the local inhabitants. Instead, much to his surprise, he discovered the group of islands that we know today as the Bahamas. Of course, Columbus is also credited with discovering America and proving that the world is round.

If you accomplished a different goal than you originally planned, then ask yourself:

How did I benefit from achieving this different goal?

As a result of this achievement, what other related goals can I pursue?

Is it still a good idea to pursue my original goal?

QUESTION TWO:
WHICH TASKS DID YOU EXCEL IN
AND ENJOY THE MOST?

"Choose a job you love and you will never have to work a day in your life."

—Confucius (551–479 B.C.),

Chinese philosopher, teacher, and political theorist

Identifying tasks you are good at and enjoy helps you set priorities for your next big goal. This is particularly important if you are a perfectionist or have problems setting and meeting deadlines. Also, as you learned in chapter fourteen, "Finding Help in All the Right Places," you can get assistance for tasks that you cannot do or do not want to do yourself.

For example, I enjoy researching and writing books. However, I need an editor to catch my mistakes, bounce ideas off of, and help me produce a clearly written manuscript. By focusing on what I do best and getting help with the other tasks, I write better books and have more fun in the process.

Here is an easy way to zero in on what you find rewarding and frustrating in your work. Divide a sheet of paper in half with the headings: "Rewarding" and "Frustrating." Then list the tasks that you excel in and those with which you would like help. After you identify the things that you enjoy and those with which you would like help, you can begin to plan how you are going to approach your next long-term goal.

QUESTION THREE:
WHAT WILL YOU DO DIFFERENTLY
WHILE PURSUING YOUR NEXT DREAM?

"The toughest thing about success is that you've got to keep on being a success."

—Irving Berlin (1888–1989),
American composer

Most successful people look for ways to learn from their successes and failures. If you want to accomplish even more of your dreams, then stick with what worked and learn from your past mistakes. As the great film screen actress Tallulah Bankhead put it, "If I had to live my life over again, I'd make the same mistakes, only sooner."

In the exercise at the end of this chapter, you will have an opportunity to rate your own performance in the various areas presented in this book. Then you can see what you will do differently when you pursue your next dream.

Pursue Your Other Dreams

"Because it is there."
—George Leigh Mallory (1886–1924),
British mountaineer, responding to the question
why he wanted to climb Mount Everest

Now that you have climbed your "Mount Everest," you probably have some other dreams that you would like to accomplish.

Take Columbus's case, for example. Once he "discovered America," he convinced King Ferdinand and Queen Isabella of Spain to fund three more expeditions to explore the coast of North America. Columbus's next dream was to find gold in the "New World."

Like Columbus, you need to identify parts of your original goal that eluded you and parts that you still want to accomplish. Complete the following statements to help determine what may be your next big goal:

Although I accomplished most of my original goals, the part of that dream I still want to achieve is:

_____

_____

_____

Now that I've accomplished my original goal, the next dream I want to achieve is:

_____

_____

_____

High Achievers Always Look for the Next Mountain to Climb

"The only limit to our realization of tomorrow will be our doubts about today. Let us go forward with strong and active faith."
—Franklin Delano Roosevelt (1882–1945),
thirty-second president of the United States

Whether your long-term goal was to clean your garage or learn how to skydive, think of each achievement as a springboard to the next. Celebrating what you have accomplished motivates you to pursue even more ambitious endeavors. Evaluating your results allows you to learn from your experience and guides you to your next long-term goal. With that winning combination, you're bound to succeed!

LITTLE EXERCISES THAT GET BIG RESULTS
Number Sixteen:
"How Am I Doing?"

Problem-Solving Strategy:
Using a Performance Rating Chart
This strategy helps you identify your strengths and
weaknesses while pursuing a long-term goal.

What's the problem? Objective self-evaluation is never easy, especially after you have accomplished a long-term goal. However, by rating yourself in critical areas you can correct your weaknesses, capitalize on your strengths, and improve your chances for success in your future endeavors.

What to do: On a scale of 0 (weak) to 10 (strong), rate your level of performance in each of the following critical areas. Be honest in your self-evaluation and answer how you actually performed, not how you wish you had performed.

How well did you perform in these critical areas?

Skill	Weak – Average – Strong
Setting long-term goals	0 1 2 3 4 5 6 7 8 9 10
Defining your motivation	0 1 2 3 4 5 6 7 8 9 10
Overcoming fear of failure	0 1 2 3 4 5 6 7 8 9 10
Setting midterm goals	0 1 2 3 4 5 6 7 8 9 10
Working on the little steps	0 1 2 3 4 5 6 7 8 9 10
Starting the project	0 1 2 3 4 5 6 7 8 9 10
Using your creative skills	0 1 2 3 4 5 6 7 8 9 10
Pacing yourself	0 1 2 3 4 5 6 7 8 9 10
Learning from criticism	0 1 2 3 4 5 6 7 8 9 10
Avoiding procrastination	0 1 2 3 4 5 6 7 8 9 10
Overcoming perfectionism	0 1 2 3 4 5 6 7 8 9 10
Meeting self-imposed deadlines	0 1 2 3 4 5 6 7 8 9 10
Finding help when needed	0 1 2 3 4 5 6 7 8 9 10
Rewarding your success	0 1 2 3 4 5 6 7 8 9 10
Addressing issues related to success	0 1 2 3 4 5 6 7 8 9 10

FOLLOW-UP

Once you have rated your performance, you can identify specific areas of strength and weakness. Your next step is to prepare a plan of action to make improvements for *each* area. You can find ways to improve your rating for each area by reviewing the specific chapter and exercises. On a sheet of paper, write the following for each area you want to improve:

Area: _____ Rating: _____

What I can do to improve:

_____

_____

_____

_____

_____

_____

_____

_____

_____

_____

_____

_____

_____

_____

_____

You can use this self-evaluation performance chart after completing any goal. When you improve the scores in the critical areas, each new goal and dream you pursue will be easier to achieve.

Little Things Checklist

Achieving a long-term goal takes commitment, planning, action, and perseverance. The following little things will also help you know what to do next.

✔ Work to make your abilities even more outstanding than they already are.

✔ Use your talents in as many ways as you can.

✔ Give yourself positive messages for achieving your midterm and long-term goals.

✔ Look for the hidden benefits that come with your accomplishments.

✔ Keep a file of your unfinished projects or unfulfilled dreams.

✔ Squeeze as much knowledge from your successes and failures as you can.

✔ Find people with whom you can share your expertise and knowledge.

WHAT'S NEXT?

Now that you have achieved your dream, you're ready to go on to chapter seventeen. Your next step is to look at all the other little things you can do to make big things happen.

17

Fifty Ways
to Make
Big Things Happen

"Actually, I'm an overnight success. But it took me twenty years."
—Monty Hall (b. 1924),
American television game show host

NOW THAT YOU'VE achieved one of your big dreams, what do you do next? What does the future hold for you? How can you and others continue to profit from your efforts? How do you know what new goals to set for yourself? How can you help others achieve their goals? How can you do an even better job when you tackle your next big goal? How can you keep from losing your perspective when the going gets tough? The following fifty suggestions can help you succeed in all your future endeavors.

1. Take another look at dreams you once thought were unattainable.
2. Maintain your sense of humor and do what you enjoy.
3. Choose to pursue a goal that you can easily and quickly achieve.
4. Finish a project that you gave up on.

5. Look for spin-off projects based on what you have just achieved.

6. Expand what you have achieved into something even better.

7. Clearly define your goals and objectives before starting another major endeavor.

8. Recall a joke someone made about your dream and turn it into a reality.

9. Pursue the goals that bring you the most happiness.

10. See how another dream fits into your other long-term goals.

11. Give yourself permission to make all the mistakes you need to achieve your goals.

12. Learn from every mistake you and other people make.

13. Change routines that waste time or don't work.

14. Improve your work habits, skills, and standards to pursue new goals.

15. Challenge yourself to build one of your weaknesses into a strength.

16. Keep your work schedule consistent but flexible.

17. Pursue your daily goals even if you are tired, not in the mood, or uninspired.

18. Be ready to take advantage of unexpected opportunities.

19. Avoid rituals that waste time and diffuse your focus.

20. Discipline yourself to ignore or eliminate distractions.

21. Look at each problem or hurdle you face as an opportunity.

22. Use all available resources to achieve your goals.

23. Consistently press toward your goal without worrying about success or failure.

24. Persevere when you reach an impasse or difficult hurdle.

25. Read plenty of books and magazines that will help you achieve your goals.
26. Write out your own recipe for success and post it where you can see it each day.
27. Tackle new goals even when your likelihood of success may be small.
28. Avoid negative self-talk that depletes your confidence and motivation.
29. Build your desire to succeed through positive self-talk.
30. Associate with people who enthusiastically support you and your goals.
31. Avoid pessimists who put you down or undermine your confidence.
32. Cultivate friendships with people who are seeking to achieve their dreams.
33. Take responsibility for what you want to achieve.
34. Don't alienate your supporters.
35. Find role models to emulate, then master their techniques and strategies for success.
36. Help other people achieve their goals by becoming a mentor.
37. Foster cooperative relationships with people who share common objectives.
38. Research the career path of others who have achieved the goals you wish to accomplish.
39. Eat right, sleep right, and stay healthy to better pursue your goals.
40. Allocate free time to relax and enjoy the company of family and friends.
41. Find productive and enjoyable ways to spend your free time.
42. Keep your successes and failures in perspective.

43. Show self-confidence and others will believe in you and your goals.
44. Identify your greatest strength and pursue it until you are an expert in your field.
45. Share your expertise with others.
46. List small and large ways to reward yourself when you accomplish tasks and goals.
47. Interview successful people and find out their secrets to success.
48. Always keep defining new goals for yourself.
49. Conceive "blue sky" projects that seem impossible except to a dreamer like you.
50. Visualize yourself living all your dreams now that you know how to turn them into reality.

Conclusion

WHAT A GREAT feeling—you've achieved a lifelong goal! It required so much hard work and persistence that you sometimes wonder how you did it. Then you remember the steps you took to turn your dream into a reality: commitment, planning, action, and perseverance.

After the idea first popped into your head, you had second thoughts about whether it was worth the effort or if you could even pull it off. After considering the pros and cons, you decided to give it your best shot and made a commitment. Then you defined your major obstacles and devised plenty of strategies and solutions. From there you mapped your midterm goals and organized the many steps necessary to achieve what you set out to do.

When you were ready to act, you took the plunge and moved forward, consistently, and with purpose. You used all your resources, tapped your creative skills, and paced yourself so that you could sustain your efforts. If others criticized your work, you learned from your mistakes and persevered. While all your efforts did not always lead to immediate success, you did not give up. You continued to push forward, overcame setbacks, and moved even closer to your ultimate destination. You reached your long-term goal because you stuck to your deadlines, looked for help when necessary, and stayed on track.

Once you realized your dream, you celebrated and relaxed. Although you remained happy with your accomplishment, you did not let your success go to your head. You kept your achievement in perspective and remembered to thank everyone who helped you along the way. You continued to look forward and aimed your sights even higher.

Your future still holds many more goals for you to achieve. The next question to ask yourself is, "Which ones do I choose to pursue?" It doesn't matter which dreams you decide to reach for, now that you know the steps to help you succeed. You know that . . . *Big things happen when you do the little things right!*

Appendix:
Problem-Solving Strategies

Chapter One: Where Do You Want to Be in Five Years?
Problem-Solving Strategy: Defining Your Objectives
This strategy helps you define your dreams as worthwhile and achievable goals.

Chapter Two: Why in the World Are You Doing This?
Problem-Solving Strategy: Making a Pros and Cons Chart
This strategy helps you zero in on the most important issues, establish their priorities, and simplify the decision-making process.

Chapter Three: Defining Your Obstacles
Problem-Solving Strategy: Making a List of Obstacles
This strategy helps you sort, classify, and identify key problems so that you can focus on solving the ones most crucial to your success.

Chapter Four: Facing the Fear of Falling Flat on Your Face
Problem-Solving Strategy: Seeing Yourself Successful

This strategy employs the same visualization techniques that many athletes and performers use to help them conquer fears and produce winning results. By visualizing what is possible, you can overcome real and self-imposed barriers.

Chapter Five: Mapping Out Your Big Steps
Problem-Solving Strategy: Developing a Midterm Goals Flowchart

This strategy helps you establish the sequence of midterm goals from the beginning to the end of your long-term goal.

Chapter Six: Organizing Your Little Steps
Problem-Solving Strategy: Developing a Flowchart of Steps

This strategy helps you organize the little steps that lead to a midterm goal.

Chapter Seven: Setting Your Plan in Motion
Problem-Solving Strategy: Sandwiching Tasks

This strategy helps you overcome inertia by combining high-interest and low-interest activities.

Chapter Eight: Tapping into Your Creativity to Achieve Faster Results
Problem-Solving Strategy: Making an Ideas Map

This strategy helps you organize many of your ideas into a visual format so you can see how they relate to one another.

Chapter Nine: Pacing Strategies to Help You Go the Distance
Problem-Solving Strategy: Making a "Hard-Easy" Pacing Chart

This strategy helps you organize and schedule easy, moderate, and difficult tasks so that you can achieve your goals without suffering chronic fatigue.

Chapter Ten: Using Criticism to Overcome Obstacles
Problem-Solving Strategy: Defining Possible Solutions

This strategy helps you use constructive criticism to find solutions.

Chapter Eleven: Twenty-One Jump Starts for Procrastinators
Problem-Solving Strategy: Making a Daily Schedule

This strategy helps you begin and sustain your efforts from the first step through the last so you can achieve your midterm and long-term goals.

Chapter Twelve: Managing Perfectionism to Get Things Done
Problem-Solving Strategy: Prioritizing Tasks

This strategy helps you overcome perfectionism by focusing on the tasks that are most important to tackle first.

Chapter Thirteen: Setting and Meeting Your Own Deadlines
Problem-Solving Strategy: Setting a Deadline

This strategy helps you accomplish a specific objective within a specified time.

Chapter Fourteen: Finding Help in All the Right Places
Problem-Solving Strategy: Using Outside Resources

This strategy focuses on seeking information, expertise, and assistance from various sources to help you find solutions.

Chapter Fifteen: Crossing the Finish Line
Problem-Solving Strategy: Checking Key Issues

This strategy helps you address five important issues before and after you achieve your goal.

Chapter Sixteen: You've Achieved Your Dream, So What's Next?
Problem-Solving Strategy: Using a Performance Rating Chart

This strategy helps you identify your strengths and weaknesses while pursuing a long-term goal.

Suggested Reading

Bolles, Richard Nelson. *What Color Is Your Parachute? A Practical Manual for Job-Hunters and Career Changers* (Ten Speed Press, first published in 1970).

Brown, Les. *Live Your Dreams* (Avon Books, 1992).

Bykofsky, Sheree. *Me: Five Years from Now* (Warner Books, 1990).

Culp, Stephanie. *How to Get Organized When You Don't Have the Time* (Writer's Digest Books, 1986).

Edelston, Martin. *"I" Power: The Secrets of Great Business in Bad Times* (Barricade Books, 1992).

Griessman, B. Eugene. *The Achievement Factors: Candid Interviews with Some of the Most Successful People of Our Time* (Pfeiffer & Company, 1990).

Jeffers, Susan. *Feel the Fear and Do It Anyway* (Fawcett Columbine, 1987).

Lazarus, Arnold, and Allen Fay. *I Can If I Want To* (Warner Books, 1975).

Peale, Norman Vincent. *The Power of Positive Thinking* (Prentice-Hall, 1952).

Shea, Gordon. *Mentoring: Helping Employees Reach Their Full Potential* (American Management Association, 1994).

Sher, Barbara. *Wishcraft: How to Get What You Really Want* (Balantine Books, 1979).

Index

Index

Index

Index

About the Author

DON GABOR is an author, communications trainer, and "small talk" expert. He has been writing and speaking about the art of conversation since 1980 and presents workshops and keynote speeches to associations, businesses, corporations, and universities. He is a member of the National Speakers Association, the American Society for Training and Development, and is a frequent media guest and spokesperson. His clients include American Express, the American Management Association, Crown Books, Marriott Hotels, MTV, New York University, Prima Communications, Random House Audio Books, Simon & Schuster Publishers, Sprint, and Viacom.

Don Gabor's full-day, half-day, and hourly workshops are interactive, entertaining, practical, and based upon proven skills and adult-education pedagogy. In addition to customizing exercises that address the challenges of your specific group or industry, he gives each participant individualized coaching in a supportive and risk-free setting. Don uses lecture, demonstration, role-playing, hands-on exercises, assessment instruments, and small group activities to create an entertaining and instructional environment where everyone attending learns the meaning of personal and professional success.

Don Gabor helps people achieve their professional, social, and personal aspirations by improving their ability to set goals and to communicate with others. He founded *Conversation Arts Media* in 1991 to accomplish this purpose.

Find out how you can arrange for Don Gabor to speak to your group about his book *Big Things Happen When You Do the Little Things Right* or his other personal development topics. You can also receive his free conversation tip sheet, "Fifty Ways to Improve Your Conversations," and more information about his books and tapes. Please write or call:

Don Gabor
Conversation Arts Media
P.O. Box 150-715
Brooklyn, New York 11215
(718) 768-0824

7 Strategies for Wealth & Happiness

Power Ideas from America's Foremost Business Philosopher

Jim Rohn

U.S. $12.00
Can. $16.95
ISBN: 0-7615-0616-0
paperback / 176 pages

"The world would be a better place if everyone heard of my friend Jim Rohn." —Mark Victor Hansen, co-author of *Chicken Soup for the Soul*

Acclaimed business philosopher Jim Rohn shows how wealth and happiness can both be yours— if you follow seven key strategies:

- Unleash the power of goals
- Seek knowledge
- Learn how to change
- Control your finances
- Master time
- Surround yourself with winners
- Learn the art of living well

This philosophy has helped millions of people find financial freedom and lead richer, happier lives. It can change your life too.

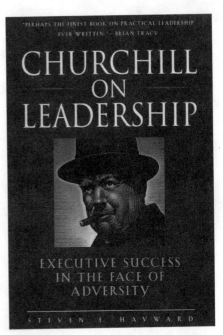

The Power of Thought

Ageless Secrets of Great Achievement

Glenn Bland

U.S. $13.00
Can. $17.95
ISBN 0-7615-0994-1
paperback / 176 pages

Within us lies the awesome power to lead, to build, to change the world. If we can dream it, we can do it. Drawing on the lives of Andrew Carnegie, Amway founders Rich DeVos and Jay Van Andel, Thomas Edison, and other super achievers, bestselling author and inspirational speaker Glenn Bland clearly and convincingly shows that with a simple but inspired return to basic values we can all achieve the success of our dreams.

Also available in hardcover:
U.S. $16.95
Can. $22.95
ISBN 0-7615-0341-2
hardcover / 176 pages

To Order Books

Please send me the following items:

Quantity	Title	Unit Price	Total
_____	7 Strategies for Wealth & Happiness	$ __12.00__	$ _____
_____	Churchill on Leadership	$ __14.00__	$ _____
_____	The Power of Thought	$ __13.00__	$ _____
_____	_____	$ _____	$ _____
_____	_____	$ _____	$ _____
_____	_____	$ _____	$ _____

*Shipping and Handling depend on Subtotal.

Subtotal	Shipping/Handling
$0.00–$14.99	$3.00
$15.00–$29.99	$4.00
$30.00–$49.99	$6.00
$50.00–$99.99	$10.00
$100.00–$199.99	$13.50
$200.00+	Call for Quote

Foreign and all Priority Request orders:
Call Order Entry department
for price quote at 916-632-4400

This chart represents the total retail price of books only
(before applicable discounts are taken).

Subtotal $ _____

Deduct 10% when ordering 3-5 books $ _____

7.25% Sales Tax (CA only) $ _____

8.25% Sales Tax (TN only) $ _____

5.0% Sales Tax (MD and IN only) $ _____

7.0% G.S.T. Tax (Canada only) $ _____

Shipping and Handling* $ _____

Total Order $ _____

By Telephone: With MC or Visa, call 800-632-8676 or 916-632-4400.
Mon–Fri, 8:30-4:30.

WWW: http://www.primapublishing.com

By Internet E-mail: sales@primapub.com

By Mail: Just fill out the information below and send with your remittance to:

**Prima Publishing
P.O. Box 1260BK
Rocklin, CA 95677**

My name is _____

I live at _____

City _____ State _____ ZIP_____

MC/Visa#_____ Exp. _____

Check/money order enclosed for $ _____ Payable to Prima Publishing

Daytime telephone _____

Signature _____